Training Women in the Martial Arts

A Special Journey

Jennifer Lawler and Laura Kamienski

GW00778319

Wish Publishing
Terre Haute, Indiana
www.wishpublishing.com

LCCN: 2006933454

Printed in the United States of America
10 9 8 7 6 5 4 3 2 1

Editorial assitance provided by Dorothy Chambers
Cover design by Phil Velikan
Cover Model: Lindsey Brodie, Lewisburg, PA
Photo by Tiffini Scott of Creative Images Lewisburg, PA.

Published by
Wish Publishing
P.O. Box 10337
Terre Haute, IN 47801, USA
www.wishpublishing.com

Distributed in the United States by
Cardinal Publishers Group
222 Hillside Avenue, Suite 100
Indianapolis, IN 46218
www.cardinalpub.com

For Jessica — jl

For my student, Alyssa, who became my greatest teacher — lk

ACKNOWLEDGMENTS

Both of us have more people to thank than space to thank them in. But we're going to try:

Jennifer

It's been quite a journey since I walked into New Horizons Black Belt Academy of Tae Kwon Do in Lawrence, Kansas almost 15 years ago. My instructors there, Donald and Susan Booth, encouraged me to become the best martial artist I could be. Grandmaster Woo Jin Jung has always set the standard for excellence. My fellow students, including Vickie and Chip Anderson, Dena Friesen, Jeanne Heitzman and Lynne Baur, helped me every step of the way. My "little sister" Chantal Anderson never gave up on me no matter how many times I failed to nail that jump spinning wheel kick. I'll miss her for the rest of my life.

Without Obi, there'd be no book. Thank goodness she had something to say.

And of course I have to thank my daughter, Jessica, for making every day worth getting out of bed to meet.

Laura

I believe that the following pages are the product of all the amazing women who have touched my life, especially the following individuals.

First and foremost I would like to thank my students. You are all truly powerful women.

I met Maureen Sherlock in 1982. She was the first person to utter the word "feminism" to me and to recognize me as an intelligent autonomous being. Thank you for removing my blinders.

I would also like to express my deepest gratitude to Ty Warren, my dear friend and confidant who has the courage of a thousand warriors and who continues to be my greatest inspiration. Thank you for sticking by me and teaching me the meaning of friendship.

I owe a great deal of thanks to my self-defense mentor Karin Sundstrom who never hesitated to criticize my work when it needed it.

I would like to formally recognize the incredible work of Nadia Telsey of *Be Free*, in Eugene, Oregon. Nadia helped me to understand that defending the heart is the foundation of all self-defense.

I have few heroes, but Andrea Tufo is one of them. Andrea is a woman of all action and little talk. My other hero is my brilliant friend Gillian Barker who has skillfully melded logic and compassion into a single organic entity. Thanks to both of you for showing me what genuine strength is.

And finally, thank you from the bottom of my heart, Prim. It goes without saying that without you there would be no book.

There have also been some amazing men in my life.

I am tremendously grateful to all of the martial arts and self-defense instructors I've had the honor to train under through the years, but I am especially indebted to my current instructor, Master Tom Merritt, who is the finest martial artist I know.

I am duty bound to acknowledge my former instructor Master Dave Burns. Thank you for providing me with a solid base on which to grow.

But of all the instructors and martial artists I've had the privilege to train with I want, above all, to express my warmest appreciation and regard for Master Doug Eaton, who embodies the essence of Tae Kwon Do with his every breath.

And finally, thank you, Don. You continuously set the standard for male supporters.

TABLE OF CONTENTS

INTRODUCTION

After attending a seminar, Laura and another high ranking female black belt knelt in the front row for a group photo. The host, a well-known kickboxing champion, flippantly announced to the group, "That's how I'd like to see all women, on their knees!"

Despite their physical training, neither Laura nor her friend had the capacity or the skills to stop the assault, which continued from that first comment. Through that experience, Laura realized that something was missing from her training and she began to look for answers. It was the catalyst to her finding a new approach to her martial arts practice, and to her role as a women's self-defense instructor.

When Jennifer was testing for her brown belt, the male judge had everyone at her belt rank line up for a pep talk afterward. The first thing he said was, "There sure are some pretty women in this group!" As if their being pretty were the best compliment he could give female martial artists working hard on their training. As if how they looked were the only thing he noticed about them. She felt embarrassed for herself and for the judge because of the criterion he was using to judge women who just wanted to be stronger and more confident.

What's remarkable about these comments is how *unremarkable* they are – how many women in the martial arts have a story to tell about sexism, misogyny and simple, misguided "compliments" in the training hall.

Laura, now the director of Kicks Martial Arts for Women, a women-only Tae Kwon Do studio in Lewisburg, Pennsylvania, recently received an e-mail from a second dan (degree) black belt in Tae Kwon Do who flatly asserted that by training without men she has "stripped Tae Kwon Do of its true meaning." Of course, this kind of arrogance is too common in martial arts, but in a very real sense he is absolutely right. Tae Kwon Do, and in fact most martial arts, were developed by men, for men. Tae Kwon Do, for example, was developed in the 1940s as a method of hand-to-hand combat training for soldiers, all of whom were men. So by opening an all-women's dojang (martial arts school), Laura has in fact taken away something essential to traditional Tae Kwon Do – men.

No one denies that women are different from men. But many deny that women are treated differently from men. That is, there is a mistaken notion that women have gained equality with men and that sexism no longer exists. Although the women's movement has made incredible advances over the past hundred years, it wasn't until as recently as the 1970s that women were permitted to train in martial arts training halls and even then they had to fight for admission and equal treatment. And in spite of gains made by the women's movement, we are still second-class citizens who experience inequality in almost every aspect of our lives. This is especially still true in martial arts, where although many women begin training, they make up fewer than 10 percent of all black belts in the world.

The field of martial arts continues to be dominated by male instructors, participants and traditions. Even though many people think of martial arts training as something that women and men, girls and boys do together, women still face many challenges because of the long history of sexism so ingrained in martial arts traditions and hierarchies.

The primary purpose of this book is to explore why this is still the case and how women can, and in some instances do, forge new traditions based on their own needs and desires. It is a kind of handbook for instructors, but also for students and supporters as well. It is necessary because women are not only different from men, but because women are treated differently from men.

Training Women in the Martial Arts is based on our experiences as female martial artists and instructors, but it is also about the experiences of the hundreds of female martial artists we've come in contact with over the years. Each woman's experience is uniquely her own. But what we have discovered is that there is also a shared experience that is common to female martial artists as a group. These common threads are woven together into the fabric of this book. Our hope is that all martial artists will benefit from our efforts.

If you're reading this, it's clear that something about this book caught your attention. Perhaps you're a female martial artist or a martial arts instructor. Perhaps you're a woman considering training in a martial art or you're involved with a woman who you believe might benefit from martial arts training. Or maybe you just liked the cover and got curious. Whatever the reason, we hope that you'll find the contents of these pages to be both informative and enlightening.

CHAPTER ONE: GETTING STARTED

Although all students, female and male, have individual reasons for training in martial arts and each has different hurdles to surmount, as a group, women have some common challenges that are important to recognize. This chapter presents a brief overview of martial arts training and focuses on common reasons women decide to train in a martial art and some of the obstacles they face when they do.

Many women who begin training do so out of a desire to learn self-defense, and many martial arts schools offer self-defense programs to students. However, it's important to recognize that, though related, martial arts and self-defense training are actually two different things.

Martial arts training is a physical discipline that includes learning techniques such as kicks and throws, performing choreographed patterns of movements to practice the techniques (called "forms" – *kata* in Japanese, *hyung* in Korean), and engaging in some form of sparring, where partners use the techniques in a structured environment to score points on one another. The skills learned in these courses can build a person's physical confidence and can certainly be used to fend off an attack. But the purpose of modern martial arts has more to do with personal growth and fitness than effective self defense, especially since effective self defense generally relies on a combination of strategies, not just brute physical force.

"Self-defense" means using strategies to keep yourself safe from physical – and to some degree, emotional and mental – harm. Of course it's self-defense to kick a mugger in the groin, but it's also self-defense to tell your husband not to speak to you like that; and it's self-defense to walk away from an argument instead of engaging in it.

Women's self-defense courses can be found in a variety of locations from community centers, high schools and martial arts studios to elaborate permanent facilities which provide regular training camps. There are many types of women's self-defense courses having no common thread other than that they purport to be "self-defense" classes and are marketed exclusively to women. These classes and seminars are as diverse and unique in approach and content as the instructors who teach them.

The most common type of unarmed self-defense courses aimed at women are combative-style courses, based on traditional martial arts techniques. One type of combative-style course, the padded attacker class, shows students how to strike and may also teach limited verbal boundary-setting skills. Eventually students graduate to fight with a mock attacker dressed in multiple layers of padding designed to protect him/her from full contact strikes. Most (90 - 100 percent) of the curriculum of these courses focuses on learning physical techniques.

Self-defense courses such as these range in time and financial commitments from free one-hour seminars to several year courses costing hundreds of dollars.

Multistrategy Models

There are many limitations and problems with the combative model of self-defense for women, which will be discussed throughout this book. We have come to recommend a multistrategy approach to self-defense, which includes learning defense strategies, assertiveness, communication skills and simple physical techniques.

Instructors who teach self-defense for women should be well-versed with regard to sexual assault and women's socialization and be able to work effectively with women and girls, especially survivors of sexual assault. One of the best ways to learn about the dynamics of sexual assault is by listening to, *and learning from*, women who have experienced it.

Acquiring the skills to teach effective self-defense for women requires no less effort or commitment than earning a black belt. Along with research and education about sexual assault, one of the best ways to get fundamental information on violence against women is through training offered by rape crisis and domestic violence agencies. This sort of free training is typically offered to volunteers. Reading and learning about sexual assault and domestic violence should be included in all self-defense instructors' training.

Instructors who are teaching without this information are severely ill-equipped and are likely to do more harm than good. Because martial arts inherently include self-defense components they are inextricably connected. This means that instructors with women students need to keep these considerations in mind. Similarly, training women in martial arts and self-defense requires an understanding of issues that may make it difficult for women to succeed.

Hurdles to Getting Started in Martial Arts

For many women, starting a martial art is a terrifying prospect. We often remind our students that the hardest part of earning a black belt is walking through the door for the first class. Laura tells them how terrified she was her first night. After pulling into the parking lot she almost didn't get out of her car! But once they start, the rest is simple. If they come to class and practice regularly, they'll be a black belt before they know it.

Everyone is nervous when they start a new activity. We're afraid of "looking stupid" and of not fitting in. We're afraid we won't succeed. These fears are magnified for many women starting martial arts training because we are not raised to use our bodies in any kind of powerful way. The movements new students are asked to perform will be completely foreign to most women. These are very real fears with very real causes. (We'll discuss these causes in more detail later on.) We try to help our new students by reminding them that these movements *are* foreign, especially for women, and that they should feel uncomfortable.

One way to help students overcome this awkwardness is to make sure students have an appropriate orientation so that they know what to expect. When Jennifer started training, her instructor met her for a few short, private lessons before the start of a lower belt class. Once her instructor had spent 15 or 20 minutes showing her the basic techniques and having her repeat them, she was asked to stay and watch the class, and was invited to jump in at any time. By the third session, she was confident enough to join the regular class. Similarly, Laura has all of her beginning students start out working individually with an instructor. Only when they begin to feel comfortable with the material are they asked to join the regular class.

Jennifer also remembers the positive feedback she got from the instructor during these early training sessions. "That's exactly it! You're doing really well!" he'd tell her. He knew that praising a student's strengths and successes helps to instill confidence in them. The encouragement kept her motivated even when she had difficulties keeping up in class. Women rarely have people who believe in them wholeheartedly and without reservation. For Jennifer, her instructor's belief that she could do it made her feel strong and powerful.

A woman's own self-image is often a huge stumbling block to training. Even with the recent proliferation of movies and media images depicting women as warriors capable of competing equally with men, a majority of women still don't think of themselves as fighters. We are raised to think of ourselves as gentle caregivers, so most of us can't envision ourselves practicing a martial art. In fact, many people still think that martial arts are exclusively for men because they believe that men are "naturally" more aggressive and that they should be able to protect women and children.

When women start training they are sometimes met with resistance from friends and family. Laura began training at age 30, but even at this late age her parents questioned her decision. After all, they asserted, "Martial arts are for men. You shouldn't do that!" Many students end up quitting because of pressures from spouses or significant others who feel threatened by their training. Both of us have had many students quit because their husbands, boyfriends or family were unhappy about their practice.

When Jennifer began training, she was in her late 20s and had the same experience as Laura – her parents questioned her decision and told her they were afraid she'd get hurt, even though they knew nothing about the training. Every time she saw them, even 10 years after she started training, they'd ask, "Are you still doing that?" Even after it had become her career. When Jennifer tested for her black belt, she invited her parents to watch her test. After she'd met the challenges, she was extremely happy about her accomplishments and knew she'd done well: she'd performed the forms with power and agility, sparred with speed and finesse, broken a small forest of boards, and passed a grueling physical conditioning test. Her father's only comment was, "You are such an exhibitionist."

There is a high turnover rate of martial arts students in general, but among female students the dropout rate is astronomical. Among other reasons we are given when a student quits is that when family finances are tight it's up to her to give up her extracurricular activities. Martial arts training is a great release and a wonderful outlet for "me time." Our students often remark that their training is the only time they have for themselves. But, since women are still the primary caregivers of children and family it is often difficult for them to make a time commitment to training. Even though women know that making time for oneself is essential to effectively care for others, too often women find it impossible to manage.

All of these barriers are difficult to overcome. But sometimes problems themselves inspire answers, and women have come up with some creative solutions to meet these challenges. Some train with their children. Others find dojangs that offer childcare. Some train with a group of women who take turns caring for all of their children. To help with financial difficulties some schools have scholarships available for students in need. Others operate on a sliding scale so that all can afford to train. Consider possible ways to make your school more welcoming to women and to help them overcome these barriers.

Why Women Train in Martial Arts

Fear: Violence Against Women

While women will often give many reasons for getting involved in martial arts – such as losing weight or getting fit or developing self-confidence – more often than not there is a desire to feel safer which underlies these reasons. To feel as if she knows what to do if she's attacked.

In the past 20 years, there has been an explosion of available information and data about violence against women. In reviewing both this data and the content of martial arts-based women's self-defense courses, we discovered an alarming disconnection between what is being taught and the reality of assaults women and girls experience. Survivors of sexual assault are stepping up more than ever to tell their stories, but most self-defense courses for women that we have reviewed do not reflect the data or the actual experiences of these women

---

What is Violence Against Women?

Violence against women is pervasive. At least one in four women will experience sexual assault in her lifetime. Most people think of violence against women as rape and battering, but it also includes less obvious violence, such as harassment, catcalls, demeaning and de-valuing language, and objectification through language and imagery. And even less obvious is what has come to be known as internal violence – promoted and perpetuated through gender training – which includes self-hatred (we're never good enough), mutilation through surgery, self-inflicted injury and eating disorders.

The fear of rape, stemming from a wide array of sources, results in women limiting their own freedom. Women are told, and often believe, that they should not and cannot go places where men can go. Women often confine themselves to home, often passing up valuable opportunities and experiences, even though, paradoxically, they are more likely to be victimized there than in public.

---

and girls. These include those courses that claim to consider current statistics and information about violence against women.

Ultimately being armed with accurate information is the first line of defense against any threat. We wouldn't go to the expense of building a flood-proof house in the desert, yet many of us still train almost exclusively to defend ourselves against psychotic strangers who jump unannounced from behind bushes. Stranger attacks do happen, the effects of which are nothing short of devastating and traumatic, but the overwhelming majority of violence against women is not committed on the street, in a parking lot or alley, nor are the assailants likely to be strangers.

Evidence shows that men are more likely to be attacked by male strangers but women face the greatest danger from men they know—often ones they love. Nearly one-third of female homicide victims are killed by their husbands or boyfriends. Ninety-two percent of women who have been raped knew their assailants, according to the U.S. Department of Justice. Women are more often attacked with intent to rape. Among other things this means that the fight will likely involve being pinned and/ or held down in some way. Oftentimes, because they are trusted, attackers are able to gain close proximity before any physical force or violence begins.

The majority of resistance strategy studies indicate that women who resist attack by using a combination of physical, verbal and psychological strategies are more likely to avoid the completion of a rape than are those who use any one strategy alone. This means that our training should go beyond merely practicing physical technique and include practicing other kinds of tactics and strategies as well. We will discuss the multiple strategy approach throughout the book.

Martial Arts for Fitness and Weight Loss

Every winter the fitness industry bombards us with advertisements around the holidays. Miracle diets and magic machines are described as the new and easy way to get fit and stay fit. Each New Year's Eve millions of women vow that this year will be the year they start a fitness program and stick to it. According to a *USA Today* study, only about 22 percent of people who establish New Year's resolutions actually follow through with them.

People fail to keep their personal promises for many reasons. One of those reasons is lack of planning; another is lack of commitment. Consumers often end up bored and discouraged after spending hundreds of dollars. Many women have trouble sticking with a fitness regimen because they embark on it with unrealistic goals. They want to lose weight fast and initially train too hard. Consequently they find the activity too difficult and/or strenuous and give up. But by engaging in less strenuous activities and by pacing activities that are enjoyable, they may be more likely to continue.

The problem rests in setting a goal of weight loss instead of a goal of fitness as a lifestyle. In order to succeed with a fitness program, the goal itself must be to make permanent lifestyle changes. In other words, the key to any weight-loss program is consistency. There simply are no miracles or magic involved in getting fit and losing weight.

Martial arts training is a great choice to help achieve the goal of lifetime fitness. Those who practice martial arts learn to set goals, make plans and develop the skills necessary to achieve those plans. In addition, martial arts are a lot of fun. No one will stick with a fitness program that isn't enjoyable. It is much easier to commit to a fitness goal and achieve lasting results if you're having a good time doing it. Martial arts have helped many develop healthy patterns that have turned into a lifetime of healthy habits.

Finding Balance in a Fitness Program

Balance is essential for a successful fitness program. Finding an activity that you like doing and participating at a moderate pace will increase the likelihood for consistency and decrease the chances of burnout. Research shows that moderate exercise is as effective as intense workouts for losing weight and improving one's overall health. The key is consistency.

Balanced Exercise

Regular exercise is a certain route to better health. However, you have to make sure that you have a balanced exercise routine involving moderate amounts of different types of exercise. Overexercising can be plain unhealthy. Here are some warning signs that you are overexerting yourself and ought to cut back: If you become overly exhausted, get frequent headaches, become dizzy, get nauseous, get very sore, cannot catch your breath, become unsteady, or your heart won't stop pounding. If you develop any of these symptoms, see your doctor to make sure that you are still in good health. Remember: the key to health is moderation!

Doing *something* consistently for as little as 10 minutes a day can have incredible results over time.

For those who enjoy martial arts or are interested in self-defense, training is a great way to get in shape. Martial arts classes can enable students of all fitness levels to work out at their own pace, gradually increasing intensity as they progress.

Getting Started in Martial Arts Through Fitness Kickboxing

After *Tae Bo* disappeared from late night TV, we asked ourselves, "Is fitness kickboxing really just a trend?" No! There has always been a fitness element to traditional martial arts. Aerobic kickboxing is nothing new and has always been considered a legitimate way of training for martial arts/self-defense.

Many women who find traditional martial arts programs intimidating enjoy and thrive in a fitness kickboxing program. This may be because many women are more familiar with dance and aerobics. In any case, fitness kickboxing can be a great intermediary step to martial arts training. After learning the basic techniques and developing confidence in themselves, women frequently transition to a more traditional training program, and feel more confident of success.

Laura has noticed that many of her students who started in her CardioKicks! program were performing techniques at green-belt level on their first night of Tae Kwon Do. Some women who are primarily interested in getting a good workout mistakenly believe that a traditional martial arts workout is easy compared to aerobics. After starting Tae Kwon Do, one of Laura's students, now a first degree black belt, remarked, "They really kick your butt! Silly me, I thought this would be easier than aerobics! Now I know better."

Effective and safe fitness kickboxing programs should be taught by trained, certified martial arts instructors. Learning the proper mechanics of martial arts techniques as well as their applications takes years of dedicated training. Experienced martial artists are uniquely qualified to teach and demonstrate them. We have seen many cases where an aerobics instructor attempts to teach a fitness kickboxing class without prior martial arts experience. This can lead to physical injury, unneces-

Body Image

Many women who are within their ideal body weight view themselves as too fat, while many men of normal weight consider themselves as too skinny. This could potentially lead to health problems because normalweight women may develop eating disorders or diet excessively, and overweight men may not think they should lose weight when they actually should. Studies have shown that overweight men were more likely to consider themselves attractive than overweight women, while underweight women were more likely to consider themselves attractive than underweight men. Maintaining an ideal body weight and healthy self-perception are important factors in leading a healthy life. Ask your physician whether you are at your ideal weight, and if not, what you can do about it.

sary stress and strain on muscles and joints, and ineffective teaching of martial arts techniques.

The other side of the coin is that an aerobics class has to have certain components to be safe and effective. These include knowledge of body mechanics and kinesiology as well as heart rate monitoring and testing. Knowledge of music tempos, safely choreographing routines and teaching to a mixed population are other areas which must be considered when teaching group fitness classes. Trained, certified aerobics instructors have a strong background in these areas. Most martial artists do not. So ideally, fitness kickboxing instructors should have a solid background in both martial arts and as group fitness professionals.

Women-Friendly Schools

A women-friendly school is a school that generally treats students in gender-neutral terms when appropriate, but that also has gender-specific self-defense programming, and takes into consideration the special needs of women. Sometimes a female-friendly school will offer women-only classes run by a female instructor but this isn't the only possibility.

Creating A Women-Friendly Self-Defense Program

Women take self-defense courses for a variety of reasons, but underlying all of them is the reality that they will face specific kinds of violence. In order to provide an effective and useful program, it's important to include the following components:

Curriculum Based on Actual Threats

To be most effective, women's self-defense programs should be created based on knowledge of actual attacks. Sexual assault and domestic violence are, by far, the most common types of violence women experience. There is certainly no shortage of statistics and information about the kind of violence women experience. Getting in touch with your local shelter is a great way to begin to become familiar with the kinds of violence that women and girls experience and how that violence is typically carried out.

Is Your School Women-Friendly?

- *How many female students are there in comparison with male students?*
- *What is the drop-out rate for women and male students?*
- *Are there female instructors? If so, are they in leadership positions, enjoying the same level of authority as their male colleagues?*
- *Notice how male and female students interact. Are female students spoken to or treated differently?*
- *Are there different standards for male and female students?*
- *Is there any noticeable bullying going on toward female students?*
- *Pay special attention to the kind of language in the school. Are there sexist comments being made? Are these tolerated by the instructor?*
- *How much contact is allowed? Required? Are students permitted to set their own contact levels?*
- *Are trained sexual assault and domestic violence advocates available at, or through, the school?*
- *Have instructors gone through any crisis training?*

The reality that women are usually assaulted by a known assailant means that self-defense skills for women should primarily include learning skills to recognize and defend against assaults committed by a trusted friend, neighbor or intimate partner. In other words, classes should account for the emotional and psychological dynamics of the common relationships between victim and perpetrator. Even while acknowledging that assailants are typically not strangers, most course activities tend to ignore the relationships and the dynamics that accompany them. In other words, commonly taught self-defense tactics – such as gouging an attacker's eyes out with your car keys – are ludicrous to the woman who is defending herself against her father or her son's football coach. Ask yourself if you could actually imagine using a particular technique against a friend or lover before thinking of teaching it as a self-defense maneuver.

Classes to Promote Self-Esteem

Self-defense classes for women should promote a woman's feelings of self-worth and self-esteem. Our culture perpetuates a kind of oppressive violence by which women learn to devalue themselves. Patriarchal culture defines the female role as one of passivity, gentleness, weakness, compliance, concern for others, and dependency. Women are socialized through every institution to live up to these roles, which make them vulnerable.

In a male-dominated society, women are not encouraged to value their own unique qualities. Instead they are defined as "good" or "bad" according to male norms and standards. These norms divide women into "good" and "bad," and it becomes an accepted idea that only bad women are assaulted. Not only is this an outright example of victim-blaming, but it also makes women blame themselves for being assaulted because they are "bad."

Of course some behaviors are riskier than others, but assault is assault no matter where a woman is or what she was doing when she was attacked. The end result of this kind of socialization usually includes feelings of low self-worth. For women, low self-worth often includes self-blame and self-hatred.

In order to defend herself, a woman must perceive herself as having value over and beyond that of an attacker. This notion goes against the very grain of women's prescribed role in society. Women are taught to be more concerned with caring for others than themselves. This "other" orientation leaves them vulnerable because it devalues them and leaves them feeling less important, less valuable than others. Women must first feel entitled to be safe and respected. This is a prerequisite for effective self-defense.

The bottom line is that self-worth and self-value are integral components of a woman's capacity to defend herself. Self-defense for women should include activities that promote and increase a woman's self-esteem and self-worth.

For example, Laura's self-defense students are each presented with an imaginary "space bubble" at the beginning of the seminar and are told that no one has the right to get inside of it without her permission. After an exercise that reveals some of our cultural norms for appropriate standing distance, the size of the bubble is determined by each student according to her own preferences for letting people inside of it. Throughout the course students are asked to be aware of their bubbles and to let anyone know if they have crossed over their boundaries. These and other activities reinforce the self-esteem and self-worth of Laura's students.

The Value of Physical Techniques

While overemphasizing the use of physical technique is detrimental to women's self-defense needs, it is nonetheless important to teach physical technique as an integral part of training. A woman must believe that she is capable of defending herself. Learning physical technique is empowering, and is an invaluable tool for increasing women's self-esteem and self-worth. Women are routinely discouraged from any sorts of aggressive behavior and have to be taught how to use their bodies to protect themselves.

Programs Based on What Women Do

Effective programs should be based on what women already do, and provide women with opportunities to practice their skills. By defining self-defense as primarily techniques of physical force, martial arts instructors have historically minimized the successful and creative actions women already use to defend themselves, often ignoring women's own strategies completely.

Anthologies like *Her Wits About Her: Self-Defense Success Stories by Women* (eds. Denise Caignon and Gail Groves) document an existing wealth of collective knowledge but are rarely considered a valuable women's self-defense resource by martial artists. Tapping into the resources and skills women already use is an essential part of teaching successful defense strategies.

Women have been successfully defending themselves for centuries using combinations of verbal and physical strategies. Women's collective experience is one of the most effective teaching resources available to instructors. As a group, women have been forced to become true masters of self-defense. Experience is the best teacher and women have a surplus of it. With proper training, development and research, instructors can begin to help women see that they already know, and often use, the most common and effective forms of self-defense.

For example, some students report that they will always drive themselves to and from a first date and pay for their meal or movie themselves. Many of Laura's college-aged students have intricate methods of "watching each other's backs," from letting dormmates know where they are going to friends watching for unusual behavior at parties.

One difficulty in laying out successful self-defense techniques is that prevention cannot be documented. It is impossible to determine how many assaults have been thwarted with a simple "No!" or refusal to engage in a conversation. But what is common to all successful strategies is paying attention to feelings of discomfort and putting one's own wishes and safety first.

Creation of a Supportive Environment

Finally, women's self-defense courses should create an environment of feedback and support. This is particularly true since many survivors of sexual assaults take martial arts and self-defense training. They can feel isolated and ashamed. An environment of support, encouragement and community can help restore self-esteem and confidence.

As self-defense instructors, we have had a remarkable number of women disclose information about their own experiences with assault. These reports have some significant common elements:

- Very few have reported that a stranger jumped them.

- The most common scenarios we hear are cases of child molestation (usually incestuous), date rape and domestic violence.
- Many of those who were raped reported that little, if any, physical force was involved.

All of the information that has been reported to us confirms that, when assaulted, women are usually assaulted by men they know. They are usually very young women or girls and are assaulted by men who are significantly older than they are. Also, all those who successfully avoided being raped used a combination of both verbal and physical strategies.

Because they work with survivors on a regular basis, advocacy workers (i.e., rape crisis counselors) are one of the best sources of knowledge about the kinds of assault women experience, as well as the kinds of self-defense strategies that are most effective.

An effective self-defense program for women should include four key elements:

- It should be based on the kinds of assault women most experience.
- It should be developed to promote assertiveness, confidence and self-worth.
- The curriculum should emphasize the skills women already use and include activities to build new skills based on them.
- Finally, instructors should be able to provide a caring environment where women feel safe to train.

Failings of Combative Models

Courses based on stranger danger fail to meet the above criteria for effective women's self-defense and are problematic in other important ways. Such models of self-defense perpetuate myths and legitimize false information, which only serves to frighten women needlessly.

Only Okay to Fight "Back"

But more important is that combative classes reinforce the notion that it is best to retaliate only when there is no doubt that a threat exists. They give "permission" only to fight back. In other words, it is only okay to fight when very clear-cut lines are drawn and a victim is sure there is going to be a physical confrontation, or after the physical assault has begun — too late to prevent it. But sexual assault is overrun with ambiguity and attempts by an assailant to confuse the victim. By focusing on scenarios with clear-cut lines of aggression, combative self-defense also serves to strengthen women's socially prescribed role as victim. These types of scenarios reject learning to rely on one's own sense of endangerment.

Assailants use tricks and ploys in many different forms. From an offer of help or apologies and reassurances to intimidation and put-downs, a sexual assailant both intentionally and unintentionally tries to manipulate his victim. The majority of assaults begin with conversation that is directed by an assailant. This conversation is intended to manipulate, coerce and confuse the targeted victim. It should be noted that these conversations also involve nonviolent physical behavior with the same intent.

Classes based on stranger assault present students with scenarios that have a clear-cut beginning, middle and end. These scenarios take a student from point A (initial contact) to point C (verbal or physical confrontation) in a predictable pattern. The mock situations presented are overwhelmingly ones in which the assailants are strangers meeting their victims for the first time.

Lack of Information

Another failing of these programs is ignorance on the part of instructors. Some martial arts instructors are unaware of the statistics about violence against women. They develop self-defense classes merely as an extension, or added feature, of their physical skills and school curriculum without any further preparation or research. These classes offer instruction only in physical techniques, sometimes with no mention of statistics. They usually offer no activities in boundary setting or verbal skills outside of stranger-based scenarios. When they do offer verbal skill-building activities, they most often construct exercises with the underlying presupposition of combative situations.

In our experience, such course curricula, drills and activities are all stranger-based street scenarios in which a student meets up with an assailant and practices a series of combative physical and verbal boundary-setting drills and strikes against him. The drills assume that the assailant is a stranger and begins his assault at a distance from the intended victim. Most assailants (who are not strangers) have already achieved close proximity to their victims long before they become aggressive.

Denial

Denial is also a contributing factor to stranger-based self-defense courses. Many martial artists acknowledge and report on the statistics and data but don't believe them or don't connect the dots between what they know and what they teach. It is in many ways much easier to deny the reality of how sexual assaults happen, to whom they are happening, and who is committing them. It's easier for both men and women. For women it's easier because disbelief enables them to believe, "THAT wouldn't, won't, couldn't, EVER happen to me." For men it's easier to accept a psychotic demonized attacker who is unlike them.

Ease

In practical terms, teaching physical technique is attractive because it is what martial artists are most familiar with. For most martial artists, teaching only physical technique is much easier than taking time to develop role-playing exercises or activities designed to uncover common obstacles women face in defending themselves. Martial artists don't need to do any extensive research or additional training to develop a self-defense course for women based on physical techniques.

It should be noted that another compelling reason to create a combative course is marketability. Combative courses prey on the fears women have. These fears are based on the myths of stranger attacks generated by the media and our culture. Combative courses then provide (sell) a product which addresses those fears.

It seems in most cases, however, that well-intentioned martial artists simply do not know how to build a self-defense class for women that integrates this information. For these and other reasons, many martial artists teaching self-defense for women accept the myth of stranger attacks and construct courses around them. Even those that report about statistics of known assailants offer little in terms of building skills that women need to confront the reality of violence against them. The skills and information necessary for women to learn effective self-defense strategies are not being offered in combative classes.

CHAPTER TWO: GENDER ROLES

A major martial arts equipment company recently introduced a new line of pink sparring gear for girls. The advertising blurb describes pink as the reigning color of "girl power." This campaign reflects a deeper trend among women and girls to try to embrace what is considered to be feminine and transform it into something powerful.

On the surface, this seems like a step forward. But digging deeper we discover that it's nothing more than an extension of telling women that it's okay to wear pants, and bring home the bacon as long as you still don a dress and high heels to fry it up in a pan. The reality is that while it's now okay for women to spar, drive motorcycles, bring home (some of) the bacon and wear blue, it's still not okay for men to cry, ride on the back of a motorcycle, be a stay-at-home Dad, or wear pink.

The idea of pink as a female color and blue as a male color is part of the arbitrary social norms prescribed to women and men in the form of gender roles. These roles affect every aspect of our lives, from how we relate to each other to our ability to defend ourselves. When we ask students to identify the qualities that make women "feminine and attractive," the results never vary. Feminine, attractive women are demure, small, agreeable, polite, nurturing, caring, and concerned with their appearance.

As martial arts instructors, we've come to understand that the biggest challenge women face in training is overcoming prescribed gender roles. Examples of effective self-defense skills and attitudes that require gender training to be unlearned include striking and using voice, assertive posture and eye contact, making assertive statements, and most difficult of all, feeling entitled to safety and to protect oneself.

Martial arts instructors often reinforce these gender roles instead of offering support in helping women overcome them. When women don't display sufficient aggression or confidence in class, instructors often try to get them to tap into their inner fierceness by asking them to imagine that they're protecting their child. Unfortunately, this merely perpetuates the belief that women should learn self-defense only because they could save other people, not themselves, with the knowledge. There is a difference between knowing you can protect yourself and your children, and believing you could, would or should only be capable of hurting others for the sake of your children.

Every day women and men are inundated with hundreds of messages about what they ought to be and how they ought to behave. These prescriptions particularly affect women and men's personal relationships. We live in a culture that romanticizes violence against women. From *King Kong's* struggling Fay Wray, Scarlett O'Hara fighting off Rhett Butler in *Gone with the Wind*, *General Hospital*'s Laura marrying her rapist, all the way to contemporary music videos and consumer advertising, romance involves women being seduced by men's force. This includes romance hidden beneath today's tough-girl façades.

The Rise of the "Tough Girl"

The idea of women conquering men is nothing new. The stereotypical beautiful woman is said to be able to bring a man to his knees with a carefully planned look. We've been told that women have had real power over men for eons. The old story was that women manipulated, schemed and connived to get and control a man. These days the conquering heroine has dropped the passive from passive-aggressive and is just plain aggressive. But no matter the method, women and girls are still taught by word, image and example that their first priority is to please men, no matter what the cost. Just how different is the story of today's kick-butt woman? Let's look at a few examples from the film industry.

One of the most lauded of the recent "strong" women films is *Crouching Tiger, Hidden Dragon*, a martial arts movie starring several of the world's most accomplished female martial artists. In one of the primary plot-building scenes, a main character, Jen, is traveling by caravan with her mother. She is seen in a stage coach playing with a hair comb when a tribe of bandits comes to rob them. The leader, a young bandit (who one might easily mistake as a current day "bad-boy" rock star), steals Jen's comb and takes off on horseback. A furious Jen, who has already demonstrated her fighting prowess earlier in the film, jumps from the coach and fights off several bandits. She steals a horse and pursues the thief. She chases him through the desert, fights with him and eventually knocks him out. Though it is never explained how they end up there, in the next scene we see Jen waking up in his cave. The bandit offers Jen food and a bath. Jen, looking very angry, demands her comb and her release. She plots to escape and eventually overtakes the bandit and runs. Her horse succumbs to the desert conditions and Jen is forced to walk. Eventually she passes out and wakes up once again in the bandit's cave. This time she is tied up. We see the bandit "caring" for his captive. Eventually Jen tries to overtake him again. They wrestle and he ends up on top of her. He kisses her and she struggles. He continues anyway. She submits and they "make love." The main message from this film, which was hailed as a victory for women, is that romance means being taken, possessed, held captive, and that no means yes – not very different from any traditional romance film.

Another popular example is the *Tomb Raider* films, for which Angelina Jolie was hailed as portraying one of the strongest female characters to hit the screen in ages. As Lara Croft she kicks butt with the best of them. Ms. Croft happens to be an expert markswoman, kickboxer and bungee jumper among her other incredible skills. She's rich and powerful and can ride a motorcycle better than Evel Knievel. Though we give her an A+ for her choice in shoes, she rarely engages in a fight in anything less (or should we say more) than spandex hot pants and pistol holsters that more than resemble garter belts. Oh, did we mention that she's drop dead (pun intended!) gorgeous? Of course she is!

What is common to all of these films is a mixing of sexuality with power, a mixture that is one of the most well known of all adolescent male fantasies. And it's no surprise that there is a double standard. It's worth noting that Stephen Seagal and Chuck Norris continue to kick serious butt into their 50s, while carrying a few extra pounds and grey hairs. But kick-butt women must forever be young, beautiful, super thin and big-breasted.

The fact is that kick-butt women films are produced for a very specific market – teenage boys. Most girls express mixed feelings about these characters and there is good reason for that. Violence against women is an epidemic. Watching women kick-butt is cathartic. We are so conditioned not to express anger that these women act as a release mechanism for us. But do we really want to glorify violence? And in the end what messages are girls receiving from these characters? It's the same old message! Sex is your most lethal weapon! It's all about men. No matter what, be feminine, ladies! Ultimately most of these "heroines" are more concerned with being sexy and finding a man to make their lives complete.

Of course, when women aren't being punished they're being forced to acquiesce. For example, the Starbuck character on the new *Battlestar Galactica* television series was an amazingly strong female character during the first season of the show. Starbuck is a fighter pilot who happens to be female. In the beginning she sported a sassy short haircut to match her no-nonsense attitude. She wore the same kind of clothes as her male counterparts and enjoyed a good cigar. After the network received a few letters complaining that she was too much of a bitch we watched Starbuck transform to a more male-centered character who is greatly concerned with pleasing her commanding officer, and finding a love interest to replace her dead fiancé. And lo and behold Starbuck now wears long hair in a ponytail.

Captain Janeway of the *Star Trek* series *Voyager* is another example from science fiction television. When we first met Katherine Janeway we breathed a huge sigh of relief. Finally a female character who was strong in, at least, a semibelievable way. Janeway is written as an assertive, capable woman in a position of authority. Yet, beneath her strength the writers found it necessary to indulge her private love of pink satin negligees and obsession-like penchant for holodeck romances in which she plays the damsel in distress.

Along with film and television images, other media, especially high fashion magazines and music videos, commonly depict women as bound, gagged, on their knees, held by the hair, grabbed by the wrist, yanked around or spread out in vulnerable positions on their backs – in other words, pervasive scenes of coercion, aggression, intimidation and fear. In the face of all this violence women and girls are still supposed to be sugar and spice and everything nice. This idea is drummed into our heads from the first time we're wrapped in a pink blanket or dressed up in a lacy bonnet and is continually reinforced over time.

The third wave of feminism has inspired a reactionary tendency to embrace any whim or fancy that a woman feels "empowered" by. It is a politics based on individualism and personal gain. Like pink sparring gear, women are being sold lipstick, short skirts and high heels as liberating. Anything is empowering as long as we want it to be and it happens to make us feel good. Advertisers and movie makers have discovered that kick-butt women fit neatly into this trend because they appeal directly to the notion of personal power. They make us feel good!

But the fact is that kick-butt women stand opposed to feminism. Their strength and appeal rests on an illusion of equality. It is an illusion that has encouraged many women to be more concerned with personal pleasure than politics. Kick-butt women breed complacency and imply that feminism is obsolete. They send the false message that girls can do, or be anything they want to be. If this were so, why aren't these young women kicking some butt?

Generation Y: We've Got a Long Way to Go, Babies!

In a recent interview, Laura was asked for her views on how the women's movement has changed young women's lives in terms of violence. In the previous section we discussed the portrayal of kick-butt women in film and how this perpetuates the illusion that young women are now adequately equipped to defend themselves. Many people believe that women in their 20s and 30s are more empowered than their predecessors were. They feel that these young women have grown up in a world that has recognized and nurtured their growth as individuals. If this were the case it would seem that courses that deal strictly in teaching physical combative techniques would be more beneficial for young women who already consider themselves to be assertive and confident.

We have had thousands of young women in our classes and have found that women in their 20s and 30s are not significantly more empowered. If young women today were more confident and assertive, it would follow that sexual assault and domestic violence would be less prevalent among this age group. But it isn't. In fact it is just as prevalent, if not more so, than ever. The fact remains that women are still an oppressed and exploited class. This means that along with earning lower wages and having fewer job opportunities violence is still an epidemic among young women and girls.

Current statistics show that at least 25 percent of college-age women have been sexually assaulted. One in 12 college-age males admit to having committed sexual acts that meet the legal definition of rape. Studies show that at least one in five middle school girls will be involved in a violent dating relationship before she graduates from high school. Two more of them will likely be in a violent intimate relationship by the time they're 24.

We have discovered that, for a number of reasons, most of the truly assertive and confident women we know are in their 40s, 50s, and 60s. Interestingly this is the point when women's risk level for violence is at its lowest.

It's true that a course focusing primarily on physical combative skills might make sense for some women, but we believe that there is no reason not to take a course that provides opportunities to develop and expand on all sorts of safety skills, especially since research indicates that it is a combination of skills that will be effective.

Film, advertising, television, pop music and other forms of enculturation still subject young women to the same kinds of mixed messages about what it means to be feminine and attractive that we were. In fact, the unattainable standards that young women are pressured to live up to leave them with as many, if not more, self-esteem problems, a weakened ability to cope, and in many cases a greater vulnerability to sexual violence.

We believe that developing healthy relationships is a primary feature of personal safety. Mixed messages about romance and relationships deeply affect how men and women interact. A friend of Laura's recently complained that he's "damned if he is romantic with a woman *or* if he treats her with respect." He feels like he just can't win! Women, he says, are an "impenetrable enigma!" In a very real sense he is right. Mixed messages result in women desiring both romance and respect. Although these are not mutually exclusive they often do stand in opposition to each other, leaving both women and men confused about how to interrelate.

Moving Past Mixed Messages

Watching a toddler grasp the concept of "mine" is incredible. Suddenly everything belongs to her. She revels in possessing her own body and all she comes in contact with, exclaiming, "Mine, mine, mine!" By around age eight, girls have all but lost this sense of entitlement.

Laura remembers the afternoon she was at a birthday party for her first instructor. He was rolling around on the living floor wrestling with two young boys. They were all having a fantastic time. A little girl, who was about seven or eight, was sitting curled up with a blanket and a doll on a chair in the corner, watching. When Laura asked her why she didn't join in on the fun, she exclaimed, "Oh no! I could never do that!" Laura realized that in spite of all the talk about equality, girls still learn to be girls and boys still learn to be boys.

In response to this, Laura has her students practice an exercise called "your body belongs to you." It consists of learning various types of releases and specific voice techniques. When a student reclaims her body after being grabbed she shouts, "Mine!"

Finding Your Voice: The Ki-hap

Hi – yaaaaaah! The martial arts shout ("ki-hap" in Korean and "kiai" in Japanese) is a guttural noise that martial artists make when performing a technique to create power.

Developing a powerful ki-hap is difficult for most women and many girls. Women are taught to be soft spoken. In fact, studies indicate that the typically higher pitch of women's voices is not entirely natural and has been artificially raised through socialization. Infantalizing women is part of our culture's gender code. Women are supposed to remain as childlike as possible. Femininity means a diminutive stature, hairless body, ponytail, a high-pitched, soft voice, and vulnerability; all childlike qualities. This self-image makes it very difficult to produce a guttural warrior yell.

A colleague of Laura's, now a fourth-degree black belt, wouldn't ki-hap in class until after she had earned her red belt – more than three years! She was too embarrassed! Before then

The Ki-hap

The ki-hap serves as a protective mechanism by essentially turning the mid-section of the body into a shock absorber. The ki-hap is also used to scare opponents, but caution should be used as the ki-hap can also tell your opponent that you are about to strike, or telegraph your upcoming move. The yell should always come from the diaphragm and not from the vocal chords. Since proper breathing begins at the diaphragm and not at the chest, the ki-hap is a great way for beginner students to focus on breathing.

she would drive up to a remote location and practice her ki-hap behind a loud radio. Eventually she found the courage to ki-hap in class and her ki-hap became well known as one of the fiercest in the dojang. It takes time to learn to ki-hap. The key is patience: instructors must be patient with their students and students with themselves. If need be, students should be encouraged to start out with a softer ki-hap just to get used to the idea. Some styles employ audible breathing with each technique. Some students are even embarrassed to breathe out loud! Once comfortable with proper breathing mechanics, students may find ki-happing less intimidating.

Gender and Contact

Advancing in the ranks, we've watched many women quit training because they were intimidated by sparring or other sorts of contact exercises. Jennifer experienced this herself when she began sparring. When occasionally she was hit hard, she had to struggle with her sense of vulnerability to continue training, and seriously thought of quitting on several occasions. In addition to her fear of getting hurt, she was afraid of hitting other people. After all, girls are forever being warned not to fall down and skin their knees, or heaven help them that they should sport a bruise! And certainly no nice girl would ever hurt someone else. Jennifer's experiences are common among many women training in martial arts.

We've discovered that most often women fear hurting others more than they fear being hurt themselves. Some claim that this is simply human nature revealing itself in play. Over the years we have noticed a consistent and quite remarkable difference in the initial levels of aggression between boys and girls. This gap narrows as girls train and gain confidence in their abilities.

We believe that girls tend to be less aggressive because they are discouraged from roughhousing at every turn. As Ellen Snortland points out in her book *Beauty Bites Beast: Awakening the Warrior Within Women and Girls,* there is no other species of animal that deliberately discourages its females from roughhousing.

I'm Sorry, I Forgot My Dress

What we're taught...
Stand right here, behind me
     I'll protect you.
Girls don't run, they scream
Don't run, you can't get away
Don't fight, he's bigger than you
Girls don't fight back
Girls can't fight back.
Girls don't hit
Girls wear dresses
Don't frown dear, you'll wrinkle
You know, you could use a little lipstick
     You look so washed out.
Stand back
     I'll do that for you.
What I've learned...
Stand right there behind you?
     I can stand on my own.
Girls don't run, they scream?
     Don't worry, you'll hear me. (LOUD ki-hap)
What? I can't get away?
     Maybe not, but I'll make you wish I had.
He's bigger than me?
     Maybe, but I'm prepared. Is he?
Girls don't fight back?
     Oh, this Girl does.
Girls CAN'T fight back?
     I don't know that word.
Girls don't hit?
     Invade my space and see.
Girls wear dresses?
     Hmm, I must have forgotten mine.
Don't frown because I'll wrinkle?
     Look at my mean face, check out my mean wrinkles.
I could use some lipstick? I look washed out?
Does this sparring bruise match my outfit?
You'll do it for me?

— By Kristen Mayfield

Aggressive, physical play is natural for both sexes in terms of developing survival skills. The fact that human girls are discouraged from playing is far from natural. Both of us have dogs and have observed that bitches fight as well as, if not better than, the males. In fact the leader of Laura's pack of five is a female peke-a-poo named Audrey. Laura often watched her teaching the puppies to fight. Audrey is a marvelously skilled fighter and instructor. Jennifer's two bitches roughhouse and tussle with each other just as any male dogs would do. However, we notice that human parents verbally and physically discourage their female children from rough play (often while claiming that the girls naturally dislike rough play), while shrugging over their boys' tussling with each other.

Helping women to come to terms with their fears and concerns about sparring and contact exercises isn't easy, but there are many activities instructors can incorporate that will help.

First, it's important not to use the "sink or swim" method of sparring. Unfortunately, it's common for students to be told to order equipment and then be put in front of another student and told to spar. Laura's first experiences with sparring were sink or swim. She remembers going home feeling defeated and considered quitting many times. On several occasions she was triggered by sparring and spent the rest of the night in tears. Laura didn't become comfortable with sparring until red belt and even then she wasn't excited about the idea. Whenever her instructor told her to put gear on, she would try to get past her fear by singing, "These are a few of my favorite things" from *The Sound of Music.* Laura had no idea that there were other avenues available to help her overcome her fears and emotional triggers and that sparring need not be a traumatic experience.

Drills and protocols that enable students to take control over their own bodies are an invaluable way to help students cope with contact. But most important is to communicate the message that students should develop the skill and capacity to articulate what they want and don't want to have happen to their bodies. This is more essential than learning how to perform a jump spin hook kick or to take a blow to the head. The ability to set boundaries is an extremely important self-defense skill that women are discouraged from developing throughout their lives. The training hall is the perfect place to practice it.

With that in mind, we require our students to establish boundaries before every contact drill. This means that each student has the right and responsibility to designate how much contact (if any) she receives during any particular drill. It also means that she can expect (maybe for the first time in her life!) that boundary to be respected. Individual boundaries will differ from class to class. This is perfectly understandable and acceptable. As a rape survivor, Laura has days where contact will do nothing but trigger her into a tail spin and end her training session. Since many women training in martial arts are rape and abuse survivors, it is important that they have the freedom, and are encouraged, to designate the level of contact they are willing to accept.

Many martial arts incorporate prearranged sparring activities. But even several months of prearranged sparring drills may not prepare a student for the experience of actual sparring. It's a good way to watch them sink, fast and hard, and to teach them to hate sparring – perhaps enough to quit. There is no need for students to feel like they're sinking.

One way Laura helps students avoid sinking is to require them to wear chest protectors for sparring. The chest protectors actually ease her students' fears about hitting someone else, not their fears about being hit themselves – those are less troubling for most female students. Even with the protectors, many students are still hesitant to hit another student. But to carry the sink-or-swim analogy a bit further, the protectors act as flotation devices and help students ease themselves into the water.

Another approach is to break sparring down into manageable pieces and give the students plenty of time to work with those pieces. For example, Laura's students are not required to buy sparring gear or the free-spar until they reach green-belt/ middle rank, which usually takes from eight months to a year. Until that time, they participate in a variety of drills and exercises to help prepare them for sparring.

One such drill is called "once and done harmony sparring." A lower-rank student is paired with an upper-rank student. The upper-rank student is given the assignment of throwing one prescribed technique at the lower-rank student. The lower-rank student is then given time and opportunity to respond by evading, blocking and counterattacking. The upper-rank student immediately throws another technique. As the lower-rank student begins to feel more comfortable, the upper-rank student will throw a variety of techniques at the same pace. This exercise helps the lower-rank student develop the vocabulary needed for sparring by giving her time to think and respond. These drills increase in speed and intensity over time until students are engaged in free-sparring matches.

Another exercise Laura requires to help her students develop boundary-setting skills is one she calls "the Southern lady handtrap." This skill is used to thwart an unwanted hug and set a boundary in a way that is assertive, nonthreatening, and even seemingly polite, as if done with a bit of Southern hospitality. As one partner approaches the other to give her a hug, the first partner gently brings the huggers hands together, cupping them in her own and politely shaking them. The entire technique ends with a handshake and a smile!

The experience of an unwanted hug, touch or comment is universal among women. Most of us have ignored it. It's our job to be receptive and polite. But a passive response is just as likely to escalate a dangerous situation as an aggressive response. The Southern lady handtrap helps students internalize that it is possible to set a boundary, to let someone know that it's not okay to touch them without their permission. Students also begin to realize that boundary-setting skills are one of the most effective tools to prevent violence from ever beginning. To put it another way, helping students to develop the skill and capacity to articulate what they want or don't want to have happen to their bodies is one of the most fundamental self-defense skills we can offer.

Of course students also need to understand that their goal is to step outside of their comfort zones. The old-school method insists that students learn to take a hit, and there is truth in this. But there is no need for any student to be pushed to the point of physical or emotional damage. The bottom line is that coming to terms with contact is a process. Learning to make demands with one's body is the most valuable skill a student can learn. Establishing boundary-setting drills in the context of martial arts training is extremely important. Students not only learn to express themselves effectively, they also come to expect their wishes to be respected.

Recognizing Gendered Behavior

It's important for instructors to learn to recognize gendered behavior. A co-instructor Laura once worked with tapped her on the nose after a sparring match and told her, "You're cute when you spar!" It's hard to imagine anyone tapping a man on the nose and telling him that he's cute when he spars, but of course Laura tapped him back and returned the compliment.

Another example of gendered behavior is hugging or kissing female students at rank promotions or other events. Hugging or kissing women is a custom that is centuries old. It is a formal expression of the idea that women belong to men and that men should have the right to touch them at will. While the custom now seems polite and acceptable to us, it is a physical intrusion that affects how women and girls perceive themselves. It implies that we are expected to comply even when we don't want to be touched.

At rank testings, Laura makes it a policy to ask each student's permission before tying the new belt on her. At every test, Laura explains that no one has the right to touch them without their permission; not Laura, not their husbands, not their uncles, nobody!

It can be difficult to recognize gendered behavior, especially when it's hidden behind norms and customs of politeness. Ellen Snortland outlines a terrific method of uncovering hidden sexism in her book, *Beauty Bites Beast,* in which she describes a kind of switch-a-roo game. Take any example of behavior and replace the men involved with women and vice versa. If the switch has no effect on how the situation appears, then the behavior is probably gender-neutral. However, if the situation seems odd or strange when switched, then it is gender-specific behavior and should be questioned. Can you imagine any instructor who would consider it appropriate to hug or kiss a male student at his promotion? Or to try to encourage a male student to hit more powerfully by telling him that he hits like a boy?

The hackneyed expression, "You hit like a girl!" is a clear example of gendered behavior. Laura's first instructor used to try to motivate her to become more powerful by telling her that she was hitting like a girl. But even with the best intentions of helping a woman to become more powerful, this expression is insulting and degrading. It contemptuously disregards the fact that girls are taught to hit feebly and not to use their bodies in any powerful way. At Kicks (Laura's school), the slogan "Hit Like a Girl!" encourages pride in our bodies, our capabilities and ourselves.

Ask yourself how it would seem if an instructor (who wanted a student to hit with more power) told a student that she "hits like a boy"? It's up to the school director to discourage any sexist remarks or attitudes about the classes.

At a recent tournament in which some of Laura's students participated, the judges decided to combine the male and female junior sparring divisions. The opening match was between one of Laura's students and a male student. One of the boy's schoolmates yelled to him from the stands that his mother had called and given him "permission" to hit a girl. "But just this once!" Laura's student went on to win the match hands down. Now imagine anyone yelling out to a female student that it's okay to hit a male student in a *sparring* match.

Conversely, a female student who trained with Jennifer mistakenly competed in the boys' junior division at a tournament. Because she was young and undeveloped and wore her hair short, no one recognized her as a girl and no one questioned her participation. She won in all three areas: board breaking, sparring and forms competition. However, when the boys found out she was a girl, they complained to the judges. She was excluded from the competition (although allowed to keep her medals) and the boys then competed among each other to find out who the male winners were. This would have been an opportunity for everyone to learn about sexism but instead what happened was immediately perceived as a problem that needed to be fixed.

Breaking down gender roles should be one of the primary functions of martial arts and self-defense training. This isn't something that can be accomplished simply by making rules and policies. Instructors must educate themselves and their students about the role that gender training plays in perpetuating and responding to violence, and be constantly aware of the gender dynamics that exist in the training hall.

Instructors must also be willing to speak out against sexist behavior or attitudes when confronted with them. This can be as simple as reprimanding a student for telling someone that they hit like a girl, to removing sexist images from locker rooms and other dojang facilities. Recently, Laura asked a friend and former colleague to remove a poster of the kickboxer who had assaulted her and her friend from one of his dojang's changing rooms. Her friend responded that it wouldn't be a popular decision, as the kickboxer had visited the school on occasion and was extremely charismatic and well-liked, especially by the younger students there.

Research indicates that many abusive men are charismatic and well-liked. But more importantly, whether or not the kickboxer was popular wasn't at issue. His behavior toward women was. Removing the poster with a school-wide explanation about believing and supporting survivors of violence would have been a much more difficult, but certainly a more supportive and pedagogic response to Laura's request.

Speaking out and taking action against sexism and misogyny not only sets the tone of a dojang, but also provide students with excellent role models.

Uncovering the Truth about Gendered Violence

Most self-defense instructors are aware that young women and girls suffer sexual abuse and intimate partner violence far more than boys and men. Unfortunately, most schools and self-defense courses offer little to uncover why this is so, or how to effectively respond to gender violence. All seem to agree that effective self-defense requires teaching students more than physical combat techniques and must include the whole story of how predators choose, lure and engage victims.

But how these stories unfold and how to respond to them are precisely what's missing from the majority of self-defense courses. Choosing at random any typical self-defense drill or scenario, you'll almost certainly find that the activity is based on a situation which has already turned violent and in which the assailant is a stranger to the victim. In fact, martial artists most commonly use the term "street defense" for what are considered to be effective self-defense techniques. This term implies that most violence occurs on the street and is committed by strangers.

When we ask students what they are already doing to keep themselves safe, we find that women spend a lot of time and effort planning ahead to avoid dangerous situations. The list of tactics always looks the same and includes parking under lights, not traveling alone at night, carrying mace or a cell phone, checking the back seat or underneath the car before getting in, and varying routes. None of these tactics is wrong or silly, but they reveal who it is that women are afraid of – the proverbial stranger lurking in the parking lot. Most self-defense courses we reviewed capitalize on these fears and invariably focus exclusively on combative techniques to be used only after an attack has turned physically violent.

As we pointed out earlier, stranger attacks do happen. When they do, they are brutal. But the overwhelming majority of violence committed against women is done by someone they know, and very probably someone they trust to some degree.

In all likelihood the initial stages of an attack won't be obvious, and attacker strategies will most often consist of ambiguous behaviors designed to gain a victim's trust and manipulate her emotions. Some of these behaviors will even seem flattering and polite. What's more is that even in the case of stranger attacks, the overwhelming majority begin with some sort of testing period during which an assailant sizes up his victim and builds a rapport with her.

We spend a great deal of time helping our students uncover the ways in which an attacker will try to build a rapport with his victim. Traditional courses almost always depict an attacker as an angry stranger, screaming invectives at his victim. But the fact is that it's much easier to attack someone who goes with you willingly. Attackers use various strategies to gain proximity to, and isolation of, their victims.

One of the exercises Laura does in her Empower! self defense program is called "get inside the head of the attacker." In this exercise, students are given a scenario in which a trusted co-worker intends to rape them. They are then asked to switch roles and become the attacker and to devise a plan to succeed in the rape. Invariably the students come to realize that their own attack strategies include:

- complimenting the victim
- gaining her trust
- asking for help
- intruding on personal space
- using other "non-aggressive" behaviors.

And in fact, these are the same strategies that attackers typically do use. Students are surprised to discover how much they already know about attacker strategies.

Most of us have, at one time or another, bought into the stranger danger myth for a variety of reasons. The media thrives on sensationalism. Stranger attacks are sensational. If the media were to report on the hundreds of thousands of rapes, assaults and molestations that occur every day among people who know each other there wouldn't be room for any other news. Because we are repeatedly exposed to sensational stories about stranger attacks, we come to believe that it is the most prevalent kind of violence. It's a lot less painful to think about a stranger attacking us than the possibility that someone we care about might harm us. When we train in self-defense, the thought of defending ourselves by actually hurting a

How Abusers and Rapists Manipulate Victims

Most rapists and abusers (whether strangers or acquaintances of the victim) will use an increasingly coercive approach to get the victim where they want her. However, the victim doesn't always recognize the coercion or feels she's overreacting (or is told she's overreacting).

- *First, they'll cross your boundaries (sit too close, touch you inappropriately, offer unsolicited information or advice).*
- *Then they will try to smooth the way by being very complimentary and developing some sort of rapport or trust. This is the most difficult kind of behavior to recognize and accept as intrusive.*
- *If you don't stop them or reject their advances, they'll go to the next stage, which is to increase their coercive behavior (telling you you're overreacting when you express discomfort).*
- *Finally, they'll isolate you from help, even saying something as innocuous as "Let's go someplace where we can talk."*

stranger is much easier to swallow than the thought of hurting an acquaintance – or a boyfriend, uncle or husband!

Gendered Advice: Self-Defense "Tips" for Women

One clear example of how the myth of stranger danger is perpetuated is a mass e-mail containing "self-defense tips and advice" that has been floating around for a few years now. We've received an increasing number of them, as well as ones about specific hoaxes such as dangers to women from abductions at malls, perfume samples that are really knock-out drugs, slashers hiding under cars, new date-rape drugs that also make women sterile, and so on.

Signs of an Abuser

The following are signs that a person is, or potentially is, an abuser. Abusers may not use all of these tactics, but they will use some of them. For help, call the National Domestic Violence Hotline [1-800-799-SAFE (7233)] or your local battered-women's shelter.

- *Extremely jealous*
- *Tries to control yoiu*
- *Calls you names*
- *Humiliates you*
- *Is overly critical*
- *Is manipulative*
- *Involves himself with you quickly*
- *Has unrealistic expectations*
- *Checks up on you or has others keep an eye on you*
- *Insists on knowing every detail of your day*
- *Reads your mail or e-mail, goes through your purse*
- *Isolates you from friends and family*
- *Is rude to family and friends*
- *Blames you for problems*
- *Displays oversensitivity*
- *Blames you for his own emotions*
- *Cruel to animals or children*
- *Abides by rigid gender roles*
- *Threatens*
- *Breaks or hits things*
- *Has sudden mood swings*
- *Angers easily*
- *Drinks or uses drugs*
- *Insists you join him in drinking or drugging*
- *Has history of battering*
- *Forces sex when you don't want it or in ways you don't want it*
- *Threatens to kill himself, children and/or you if you leave him*
- *Strikes you in any way*

One of the more ridiculous e-mails warns women never to wear overalls or a ponytail! Another forbids women to balance their checkbooks in their car! When we work with groups, we have to spend a great deal of time debunking this sort of alarmist (mis)information.

The types of scary stories found in these lists of "tips" are everywhere and seem to be increasing. They are successful because they play on the existing fears of women. More than that, they reinforce gender roles by implying that women can't take care of themselves; women must stay safely indoors; and women who venture out into the world, especially alone, will be punished with rape or other physical assault.

Of course staying home alone is also taboo for women. Jennifer belongs to an online group where women talk about balancing their many roles in life. One of the most common requests for help has to do with staying safe. Leslie, for example, recently wrote, "Do you answer the door when you're home alone?" Of course Jennifer does. How else would the plumber access the sink that needs to be fixed, or the UPS carrier deliver the package that requires a signature? Many women live alone, but some of these lists of tips would make it seem as if that's the most dangerous situation in which a woman could be.

Ironically, being home is one of the most dangerous places for a woman, but it's not the stranger at the door who's likely to be dangerous – it's much more likely the man she's living with. Alarmist fears are perpetuated in order that women feel the need to depend on "trustworthy" men for protection, when the unfortunate truth is that it is most often men we trust from whom we need to be protected.

While there are some bits of useful self-defense strategy scattered throughout these otherwise insulting and inaccurate lists, such as increasing awareness and using confident posture, these sorts of "stop," "don't," "always" and "never" commands serve primarily to strengthen myths and perpetuate a system of victim blaming and survivor self-blame. They imply that women are incompetent and incapable of making good decisions. They tell us that if we follow the rules — stay home, travel in packs, dress accordingly — we'll stay safe, if we don't we're an easy target, and when we're attacked it's because we didn't do what we "should" have done. They either don't address, or only make mention of, violence against women as it most commonly occurs. Theses lists are designed to keep women off balance and fearful. When women are fearful they will be reluctant to challenge the power structure. They will stay "safely" inside the house.

Of all the bits of advice offered by these lists one of the oldest and most dangerous is the adage that a woman should always comply with her attacker. It's important that instructors stress that any escalation of an attack will increase the risk of physical injury. As soon as physical or verbal resistance begins, for example, there will be an escalation.

However, a passive response, such as compliance, will also escalate a situation. Compliance unwittingly offers an attacker a kind of green light to continue his attack. Consider cat-callers for example. We are told that they are really just "boys being boys" and the catcalls are a kind of "compliment." (We don't understand how it is that a compliment should make us feel so lousy!) But even though we feel terrible, many of us ignore the catcaller, who then continues to harass us. In essence the situation has escalated. When we ignore him, the catcaller feels empowered to continue his behavior, either toward us or toward his next victim.

However, it's vital that we help our students understand that compliance *has* been used successfully. Compliance is most often a viable self-defense technique when used as part of a larger strategy and in addition to other resistance tactics. But compliance alone will almost always escalate an attack. This does not mean that if one chooses to comply then the attack becomes her fault. Responsibility for an attack always rests solely with the perpetrator who decides to commit violence in the first place.

Gender and Self-Defense: Designing an Effective Course for Women

Considering that breaking down gender roles is essential for effective self-defense training for women, and that there is usually some sort of pre-existing relationship between attacker and victim, and that assaults typically begin with nonaggressive manipulation tactics, the question must be asked: What sort of self-defense skills would most effectively thwart violence? What kind of activities and scenarios need to be included in a self-defense course for women?

To begin, an effective self-defense class for women should include developing skills of awareness. But what exactly is awareness? Because of the strength of the myth of stranger danger awareness is usually thought of as being attuned to your surroundings. This is an important part of awareness, but awareness is much more than that. It's learning to pay attention to that little voice inside your mind that tells you something isn't quite right. It's giving serious weight to the nagging feeling that tells you he's too polite, too nice, too friendly, or giving you too much information. Awareness is being conscious of feeling uncomfortable when answering a question or responding to a request for help. It's this sense of awareness upon which effective courses for women need to be built. This means that along with physical skills, courses should include activities designed to help students recognize and defend against the ambiguous intrusions leading up to physical assault.

One exercise Laura facilitates in her self-defense workshops is called "don't pick up the rope." This example helps students recognize their protective inner voice and develop an awareness of how attackers look for openings by throwing out verbal ropes for his victim to pick up so he can pull her in. He may try to push her buttons by insulting her, but more often he will try to compliment or agree with her to gain her trust.

It is also recommended that students practice "the broken record" technique, in which the student repeats a non-invitational refusal to engage with her attacker. For the exercise students are separated into groups of three. Each is given an index card and asked to write down two topics that they feel very passionate about. These will range from vegetarianism to abortion rights. Once the students have their topics, they exchange cards with a neighbor. Each member of the group is given an assignment. The first is the designated "attacker," the second is the "defender," and the third is the "witness."

The defender is given a phrase to repeat as if she is a broken record. It's important that she has already had the opportunity to practice controlled breathing, assertive voice tone and eye contact. The attacker's job is to persuade the defender to say something other than her broken-record phrase, using either a positive or negative approach. The witness is given the task of keeping a record of fluctuations of the attacker and defender's voice, body language and broken record phrasing.

Invariably, students remark on how emotionally stressful the role of defender is and how difficult it is not to respond. Laura has noticed that no matter how often she, herself, participates in this activity with her students, she always gets a bit hot under the collar when asked to defend herself.

Interestingly, students also report that being the attacker is just as stressful and that they find themselves changing tactics in response to the defender. Witnesses notice nervous responses such as rapid breathing, reddening faces, fidgeting, lowering of eyes, giggling or smiling, arms folding, and moving back.

Along with activities to promote awareness, courses should also include activities that uncover how traditional gender roles encourage women to be thought of, by both sexes, as easily targeted victims. Courses should also explore gender-specific dynamics involved in the personal relationships between victim and assailant.

An exercise designed to reveal just how deeply gender roles affect us asks students to describe a woman who is attractive and feminine according to our cultural standards. Invariably the description includes adjectives such as passive, dainty, small, thin, dependent, polite, easy to get along with, nurturing, selfless, very concerned with her appearance, weak, helpless, and so on.

The students' next task is to describe an unfeminine, unattractive woman. This woman is aggressive, bold, opinionated, selfish, big, strong, muscular, careless about her appearance, rude, independent and so on. If we look at these lists side by side and consider which woman is better prepared to defend herself, we immediately see that the unattractive woman would fare much better.

The second list includes many of the attributes that would describe a masculine, attractive man. It's important to help students realize that none of the qualities on either of these lists is inherently negative. In fact, in our minds a truly kick-butt woman (and kick-butt man!) would possess all of these qualities along with the capacity to access them when appropriate. The problem rests with the fact that women are pigeonholed into one side and men on the other. This is not only stifling, but creates an imbalance in power and is a recipe for violence against women.

In all of our course offerings, instructors need to remember that women are under a lot of pressure to be good victims. It's up to instructors to help female students unlearn harmful gender training and to develop resources to resist this pressure. Instructors can do this by providing responsible martial arts curricula and self-defense courses that uncover how gender training, hierarchies and power dynamics affect women's ability to train, perform and defend themselves successfully.

For example, Laura has a rule in her dojang that students should avoid using the phrase, "I'm sorry," because women too often apologize for things that aren't their fault and blame themselves for matters not under their control. Laura often remarks jovially to her students that she has seen women apologize to a wall after bumping into it! Of course, there is nothing wrong with apologizing when you make a mistake and hurt someone, but women tend to apologize for their own existence. Laura's rule is designed to help students begin to apologize only when there is good reason for it.

Oftentimes a female student's biggest obstacle to training will be self-castigation. Women are notoriously hard on themselves. Consequently many women have an even more difficult time accepting praise than criticism. There seems to be a little voice inside our heads telling us we're just not good enough. That voice has convinced many a female student to give up training. Laura remembers her green stripe test, at which she won a medal of honor for her *hyung* performance. Laura felt that she shouldn't have even passed the test let alone have won a medal for her performance. After the test, she sat in the parking lot crying and swore she'd never return because she was too embarrassed. Her instructor quipped that at gold belt she wasn't the best judge! But Laura's unintentional arrogance aside, she simply couldn't quiet that inner voice that kept repeating she just wasn't good enough.

To confront this issue, Laura has incorporated several verbal exercises as regular features of her students' traditional Tae Kwon Do training. For example, Laura often pairs up her students up to perform *hyung* (forms) for each other. The obvious purpose of this drill is to help students get over the jitters of performing on their own while being watched closely. But Laura has taken the drill a step further. While observing her partner, the first student makes mental notes about her partner's strengths and weaknesses. These notes must be detailed and specific. This drill helps the observer learn to articulate facts and concepts about good technique, thereby deepening her own understanding. The observer then relays these facts to her partner, who has been instructed that the only permissible response is, "Thank you." Nothing else!

Laura developed this exercise after observing that when her students were critiquing each other's form, a large discussion, mostly driven by ego and the little voice we talked about earlier, would ensue. Laura felt there was a good opportunity for serious self-defense work hidden beneath these discussions.

Attackers will often use tactics of compliment or criticism to elicit responses from his intended victim. This drill helps Laura's students to accept comments they find meaningful and discard those they don't. It also gives them an opportunity to practice responding in a controlled non-escalating manner. Although none of Laura's students mean the others harm, it is difficult for many students to accept criticism and praise without responding. But a response is just what a potential attacker is hoping for. He is throwing out an emotional rope, hoping she will pick it up and give him the opportunity to pull her in. This drill gives students a chance, within the context of traditional training, to practice letting go of the rope.

CHAPTER THREE: POWER DYNAMICS

Power exists when one person has some sort of an advantage over another. Kinds of power include physical, emotional, economic and social. Some power relationships are well-defined. The formal ranking structures found in most martial arts are good examples of clear-cut formal power structures. More often power structures are less explicit. They are embedded so deeply in a culture or organization that they become invisible because they seem normal.

Correspondingly, disproportionate power is obscured in situations where certain types of behavior are considered natural, polite or correct. For example, the concepts of femininity and masculinity are so deeply entrenched in our culture that the power relations they define seem normal and natural to us. But although there are natural differences between men and women, femininity and masculinity are codes of behavior which are socially constructed and serve to authenticate the power of men over women.

Although the women's movement has narrowed the power gap a bit, the fact remains that men have a distinct advantage over women. Most often this advantage is thought of as physical – i.e., men are bigger and stronger than women – but the reality is that the practical power men wield over women has little to do with any kind of physical advantage. Because we live in a patriarchal culture, men hold economic, political and social power over women at every level. This power extends to our personal relationships and does not disappear simply because we wear a unisex dobok and line up according to rank. In fact, social power disparities often become even more pronounced in systems of strict hierarchy, such as are found in martial arts training halls.

Many women begin martial arts training hoping to become empowered. We don't know any female martial artist who doesn't feel she's been empowered through her training in some way. But it's important to keep in mind that women and girls are taught from day one to be deferential. This gender role training leaves us particularly susceptible to the misuse of power that strict hierarchical structures can encourage.

Training in a martial art can include rich emotional and spiritual aspects, and a strong bond often develops between instructor and student. When this relationship develops with mutual respect and compassion, it is beneficial for both teacher and student. But the student-teacher bond can complicate already uneven power dynamics and leave a student extremely vulnerable, especially if a student has low self-esteem.

Because so many female martial arts students are struggling with self-esteem issues, it is vitally important that instructors recognize the enormous influence they have. In order for training to be practically empowering, students must be given ample opportunity to develop their own physical and mental power and authority.

Bullies / Rescuers / Supporters

Women's entry into the training hall, or any male-dominated field for that matter, provokes one of three general responses in men. They will tend to bully, rescue or support.

The Bully

The bully is the guy who thinks that the training hall is a sacred male domain, that it isn't natural for women to fight, and that any woman daft enough to try it should be put in her place. How aggressive he gets largely depends on how much his instructor will permit as well as the overall atmosphere in the training hall. Keep in mind that a bully might not realize there is anything wrong with his behavior. He is simply doing what seems normal to him.

Bullying can be either obvious or subtle. Subtle bullying comes in the form of sexist, demeaning remarks while training. Laura's experience with the kickboxer (in the Introduction) is a case in point. Other types of remarks might include focusing on a woman's appearance rather than her performance (as happened with Jennifer). He may question her "femininity." Or he may tell her that she "hits like a girl." Bullying may also include inappropriate touching such as groping.

Judges at tournaments may dismiss female athletes and give them poor marks. The most aggressive bullies will try to physically intimidate female students, sparring too hard in matches or self-defense exercises. Since women don't grow up rough-housing, and in fact are discouraged from doing so, these experiences can leave a female student feeling frustrated at best, and at worst, feeling so overwhelmed that she quits.

Jennifer encountered a bully early in her training. Since he had been training a lot longer than she had, he was more proficient in sparring. Every time they sparred together he would aggressively score as many points against her as he could. Instead of trying to teach her anything or help her become a more competent sparrer, which is the point of practice, he had to prove, over and over, that his skills were superior to hers. At the same time, he would roll his eyes and sigh loudly at her inexperienced attempts to block or counter his attacks. Needless to say, it was an extremely demoralizing experience for Jennifer. She certainly celebrated when he left the dojang.

Conversely, she encountered many men (and women) who were superior in skill but did not feel the need to bully her. Instead, they took the time to train her and educate her about effective sparring. Those matches were much more fun, rewarding and worthwhile – for both fighters.

The Rescuer

The rescuer is the knight in shining armor. He is chivalrous and gallant. His intentions are always good, but the results never are. He is the guy who welcomes women into the training hall because he can "help" them. He thinks it's fair that women be "allowed" to train with men and that they *should* train with men. Women may hit like girls, but he can "fix" all that.

According to the rescuer, women should be placed on a pedestal, and it's up to him to help keep her there (pure and unharmed) as well as to teach her how to stay there without falling off. Unfortunately being on a pedestal is just as restrictive as being bullied into a corner. Rescuer behavior is much more difficult to recognize, because a lot of it seems normal (and even polite!) to us.

Laura once had a rather bizarre encounter with a rescuer who, while co-teaching a prearranged sparring drill together, said to a young male student training with a young woman, "Oh, and you should never hit a woman!" When Laura asked why, he replied, "Well, in case she's pregnant!" Although Laura wanted to ask him how the young female student was supposed to train effectively if her partner refused to hit her, instead she asked him what the rule would be in her case since she happened to have had a hysterectomy some years ago. He didn't seem to have an answer!

In addition to his statement relegating the female student to a position of importance below that of a potential but nonexistent fetus, it disregarded the fact that a pregnant woman may be called upon to defend herself, and that men have even more vulnerable reproductive organs. What's more, pregnant women in this country are more likely to be the victims of a homicide than to die of any other cause. Laura has often wondered how this instructor would advise women who are pregnant to defend themselves. She also wondered what he'd say if he learned that the first student Laura promoted to black belt was pregnant during her examination.

Despite the trend of so-called kick-butt women, we are still repeatedly told and often convinced that we must wait for and encourage the benevolence of men to guarantee our personal safety and to end violence. This strategy is an example of waiting for the knight in shining armor to decide the fate of the distressed damsel. It reinforces the idea of women's incapability of self-defense and self-determination. Many times this attitude will be articulated in statements of concern. A rescuer might discourage a woman from doing an activity she wants

Training While Pregnant

Like many female martial artists, Jennifer continued training while she was pregnant. Because one of the female instructors in her school had continued to teach up until her ninth month, no one was particularly surprised or concerned when Jennifer said she intended to continue training as far into her pregnancy as she could.

However, Jennifer did have to educate her fellow students. Most seemed under the impression that she had somehow suddenly become completely fragile. Consulting with her obstetrician, Jennifer learned that she could continue training almost exactly as she always had, because nature had made sure that developing fetuses were well-protected by a woman's body. In fact, because she felt more vulnerable during her pregnancy than she'd ever felt before, continuing training reassured her that she could take care of herself even when she was nine months pregnant and moving more slowly and awkwardly than usual.

Jennifer was also pleased to learn that several other students who became pregnant after her were inspired by her example and continued training during their pregnancies as well!

---

to do, and is competent at doing, because he feels it is too dangerous for her.

Jennifer recalls one rescuer who asked her if she was concerned that teaching women self-defense would give them a false sense of security. In other words, sure, women can train but it won't help them defend themselves against an attack. Again, the implication was that women are incapable of self defense. Jennifer pointed him to two recent local news items where they lived where in two separate incidences women had driven off attackers. In the first case, the woman merely shouted at the attacker and he fled; in the second case, a woman shoved the attacker aside and escaped to safety. Both women were unharmed. But if they hadn't tried to defend themselves, they most certainly would have been mugged or raped.

At a self-defense course Jennifer organized, a male co-teacher told the assembled women students that they shouldn't use their self-defense skills to get into trouble – the implication not being that they would provoke bar fights, but that they would use their skills as a license to do things like walk by themselves after dark. Again, the belief here is that even if a woman trains, she isn't actually capable of defending herself and still needs a male escort after dark.

We have both had many conversations with male martial artists who say that women wouldn't "have" to train if only men weren't so violent. The fact is that *no one* would have to train if men weren't so violent. Of course reducing violence is a worthy goal, and we believe that one day men will stop raping. But to propose that the best safety strategy for women is to leave it up to men to decide not to attack them perpetuates the idea that women must depend on men for their safety. Training should encourage women to secure their fate in their own hands and help them to learn to be their own rescuers, heroes and knights in shining armor.

The rescuer rarely realizes he is undermining his students' training. But, whether unintentional or not, saving your students, or doing it for them, isn't helping them. Laura has a beautiful poster on the wall of her school, which pictures a female martial artist in a blocking position. The headline reads, "Confidence Comes from Trying." It's not only bullies who prevent women from trying. Because the rescuer habitually (and politely) intervenes, many women don't get the chance to try.

Laura remembers a well-meaning father of some girls in her dojang who wanted to help some of her adult students move a heavy bag from the closet. Laura discouraged him from doing so because she didn't want her students' autonomy to be undermined. His willingness to help may or may not have been based on a belief that the students were incapable of moving the heavy bag on their own, but no matter. If he had helped, the result would have been the same. The students wouldn't have had the opportunity to succeed on their own.

Rescuer behavior legitimizes the idea that women need to be "helped" and is exactly what leaves us believing that without men we would be rendered defenseless. It is as sexist and destructive as any other form of misogyny. Instead of reinforcing the notion of being rescued, effective martial arts and self-defense training should foster and encourage self-determination for women, both as individuals and as a group.

The Supporter

We talk more about ways to support women martial artists throughout this book. For now, a couple of brief stories will illustrate the point. A student who took Laura's self-defense class was coming out of a department store one night carrying some packages. Like many students she was on high alert after taking the course. She was scanning the lot, had her keys in her hand and was heading toward her car when she noticed that a man was casing her about five yards behind. She turned and looked at him and continued walking. He continued to follow her so she changed her path slightly, still heading for her car. When she got to her car he was still there. She dropped her packages, turned and yelled, "BACK OFF!" The man jumped three feet in the air! It turns out his car was next to hers! She was very embarrassed and apologized. The man told her that he thought what she did was wonderful and that he was going to tell his wife and daughter about it.

Though this story exemplifies just how deeply the fear of strangers in parking lots runs, it also illustrates that *the good guys will understand!* In this instance, instead of showing offense at being accused of following her, the man in question understood the woman's fear and validated her response. It also means that a good guy will respect a "No!" no matter what the situation. Laura reminds her students that any man who doesn't respect their boundaries and wishes isn't worth hanging around. If he's a good guy, he will understand! There are lots of good guys out there!

Training Women in the Martial Arts

A mother of one of Laura's red belts expressed some concerns about her sixteen-year-old daughter taking her Empower! class. Laura requires her students to take Empower! before testing for black belt, because she feels it offers them a chance to work on skills that aren't always appropriate to practice within the context of traditional martial arts training. The mother told Laura that she was afraid her daughter would get the idea that all men are out to get her.

This is a variation of one of the most common objections to any kind of feminist thought—accusations of being a man-hater. Laura explained that while there are certainly many good guys out there, the truth is that there *are* also a lot of men out there who are out to get her. The incidence of rape and battering in high schools and on college campuses is staggering. Gavin DeBecker, author of *The Gift of Fear*, got it right! To arm her daughter with accurate information, so that she will have a healthy sense of fear, is one of the most valuable gifts the mother can give her. Shielding young women from the reality of rape and abuse will only leave them with unfounded fears, false senses of security, and more vulnerability. Encouraging young women to uncover the truth about violence is one of the most important jobs of the supporter.

The supporter realizes that women experience violence in very specific ways. But instead of trying to keep her safe, he encourages her to keep herself safe. He isn't threatened or offended by her independence, skill or strength. He respects it. When Laura first opened Kicks Martial Arts for Women, she had many decisions to make. She kept asking her husband for advice, but he invariably refused to get involved. His stance was that none of these decisions should be his; they should be made by women. His support helped Laura grow as a leader and acknowledge her own authority. The good guys will understand and they will back off.

The deep-seated images of man as rescuer and woman as rescuee are a small, but integral, part of the systematic socialization process that defines what it means to be women and men in our society. This socialization is not accidental or arbitrary. Gender roles serve a specific purpose. Along with being an effective tool of political oppression and economic exploitation, gender training leaves women vulnerable to violence and encourages men to seek control and power.

Women have just as much difficulty recognizing these gendered concepts as men do. Jennifer once sparred with a young male student, a very fit National Guardsman who had only been sparring for a few months. By that time, Jennifer had been sparring for 10 years. She scored several points on him and took the time to show him how to react to her techniques. He was excited to learn some new blocking and countering techniques and they had an excellent talk after the session. However, the young man's girlfriend, who had been watching the class from the sidelines, was embarrassed and humiliated on his behalf that a woman had beaten him in sparring. That was all she could see; she wasn't able to understand that skill comes with practice and learning, and that a man can't innately defeat a woman with superior skill just because he has a Y-chromosome.

Physical Power

Most people believe that men are bigger than women. They also believe that this gives men an advantage in a physical fight. No martial artist worth her weight in salt will deny that size can be an advantage in a physical encounter. But the media portrayal of men and women would have us believe that the world consists exclusively of 300-pound football players and 90-pound cheerleaders. Even when we realize that this is a gross exaggeration, most of us believe that men are generally bigger and stronger than women. Since accurate information is the most powerful self-defense weapon, it makes sense to explore just how accurate our conception of the size differential between men and women really is and what the ramifications of these beliefs are.

On average men are, in fact, bigger than women. But what does that really mean? It simply means that when you gather a random sampling of 100 men and 100 women and line them up according to size, the smallest 20 people will most likely be women and the largest 20 people will most likely be men. So the average size of men is bigger than the average size of women. But what is glossed over here is the fact that *80* of these women will have a male counterpart approximately her size. This 80 percent overlap in size actually reveals that we're not that small and they're not that big.

The football player–cheerleader image runs so deep that we believe it ourselves and set goals to achieve it. Women have a distorted view of body size. This belief has us dieting to the point of starvation and lies behind the epidemic of eating disorders from which women suffer. But remember, it's not just ourselves we see as being bigger than we really are when we look in the mirror. When we look at men, we see them as being bigger than they really are as well. When we ask women to consider all the men and women they know and how big they really are, we always get a reaction of surprise. In addition to the exaggerated natural gross size disparity between men and women, we learn to believe that we are supposed to be small and men are supposed to be big. To be feminine means to be small.

Over the years, we've repeatedly heard comments from clients and students such as, "I don't want to bulk up! I don't want to get big!" Interestingly, in this context bulk refers to muscle, which translates to strength – yet women feel compelled to avoid it. The drive to take up as little space as possible has us following starvation diets and having dangerous plastic surgeries, and has led to an epidemic of eating disorders.

As a group fitness instructor, Laura noticed that the fitness industry takes advantage of these insecurities. In her *CardioKicks!* fitness kickboxing instructor's certification course, Laura stresses the importance of de-emphasizing weight loss and emphasizing strength. Phrases which are common among group fitness instructors such as "Bikini season is coming up," "Think about your favorite outfit," "Think about the mini-skirts when you go out dancing," are forbidden in *CardioKicks!* Instead, words like "strength," "power," "stamina," "mighty" and "healthy" are used as motivational words.

In our society, women are also encouraged to have small posture: legs should be crossed, heads and eyes lowered and shoulders slumped . The deliberate encouragement of unhealthy small bodies and submissive posture renders us weak and vulnerable.

Instructors need to be aware that most women believe they are smaller, weaker and less physically capable than men, and their "inferiority" is a natural condition. They may believe that they will always be at a disadvantage, even with the best of training. It is up to instructors to help students gain an accurate picture of the relative size and strength of men and women. This means avoiding comments that legitimize the myth of size disparity and consciously making positive statements regarding a student's strength and size. Instructors should formally encourage female students to strength train and to extol the beauty of strong female muscle. If possible, have training equipment available for your female students to use, while keeping in mind that most of them have probably never touched a barbell in their lives. This means you should be able to show your female students proper lifting technique and help them past their fears of inadequacy. Schools with women students should also have resources available for women suffering from eating disorders and body image problems, and instructors should receive at least rudimentary training in dealing with crisis situations.

Though the average-sized women is not as small as we would believe, it's important that when a student is smaller than average we address her specific needs and challenges. This means helping her to train to her strengths. Laura encourages her smaller students to practice staying in close in sparring or self-defense exercises. Even though it is a more uncomfortable place to be, it offers smaller students a great advantage.

Social Power / Authority

In order for a physical assault to succeed, an assailant must have power over his victim. We usually think of this power as being physical power, but the fact is that most assailants wield a very different, even stronger kind of power over their victims – that of authority, or social power.

Culturally and politically, men are in power and therefore have authority over women. Men tend to dominate spaces; they learn to be in control. Both of us have watched the responses of groups of women when a man "joins" the group. Women who had displayed open and relaxed body language tighten up and shrink. Nervous gestures like hand wringing, hair twirling and pen tapping increase. Eyes, once focused and alert, drop to the floor. Women who were speaking freely either stop speaking or become stammering and hesitant.

Authority comes in many forms. It can be officially sanctioned, such as that granted to the police or government officials. Authority can also be job-related, age-related, or credential-related. Any kind of mentoring relationship implies authority – for example, coaches and athletes, teachers and students. Most of these relationships are healthy. But unfortunately, any relationship that has a wide gap in authority has the potential for abuse. It's not surprising that so many assaults against children and teenagers are committed by adults in authoritative roles, including some martial arts instructors. Likewise the fact that men hold social and political authority is an underlying reason for the pervasiveness of violence against women.

Historically, women's bodies have belonged to a man or men: a girl belonged to her father and a woman to her husband. Complex laws existed for determining to whom a woman belonged should a husband, father or brother not be available. One infamous example is the *droit du seigneur*, or the right of the first night, which gave each medieval lord the right to take first sexual access to any female serf who married on his land holdings. These laws made raping new brides legal during the Middle Ages. Our own legal system still favors the perpetrator while blaming the victim.

The well-publicized Kobe Bryant debacle, in which an NBA star was accused of rape, is a clear example. The dismissal of charges against Bryant was the result of a concerted campaign to blame his victim, including the disclosure of her identity. Another example of our culture's tolerance of sexual assault was the episode of attacks in Central Park, New York City during and after the annual Puerto Rican Day parade in June of 2000, in which over 50 women were groped and harassed during booze-fueled, postparade partying. The media coverage focused on how the women were "asking for it" and how they were "dressed provocatively." This case reminded Laura of another one she heard about at a feminist workshop. A 12-year old girl was raped in a park in Chicago on a sweltering 103-degree summer day. Her rapist was set free because the girl was wearing shorts and a halter. Jennifer's community was outraged when a local judge told an adolescent girl raped by a group of men that she had contributed to the attack by drinking alcohol with them. The rapists, though convicted by a jury, were given probation by the judge.

Because of the heroic efforts of the women's liberation movement, many overtly sexist laws have been changed in the United States; some just within the last couple of decades, such as the requirement of parental or spousal permission to obtain an abortion. Yet as a class, women are still dependent on men financially, politically and socially. Our bodies are objectified and presented as simply another thing to be controlled by someone else. They don't belong to us.

The amount of physical property women own is negligible in comparison to men. Women comprise more than 50 percent of the world's population, yet we own only one percent of the world's wealth. Women occupy an extremely small percentage of power positions such as corporate boards of trustees or political offices, and women and children are the most impoverished group in the world. Those of us who do manage to secure positions of importance are constantly reminded to shape up, fly right and play by the (patriarchal) rules. But even when we do fly right, we inevitably crash against a glass ceiling.

Organizations in which women occupy equitable leadership positions and power are almost nonexistent. This is especially true in martial arts and self-defense. The illusion that women have "made it," and are now equal with men naturally extends to martial arts training. The fact that women are involved in martial arts at all has led some to believe that women are equally represented. But since most martial arts were invented by men and for men, they are still organized under "traditional" (read "male") guidelines. Correspondingly, most martial arts organizations are still run by men and have predominantly male membership. As mentioned above, fewer than 10 percent of black belts are women and even fewer occupy roles of leadership in martial arts organizations.

In the dojang in which Laura rose up in rank there were no women in leadership roles. Women were assistants, usually helping with the kids classes or teaching aerobics classes. In Jennifer's school, the co-owner and co-head instructor was a woman, but she was in a junior position to the male co-owner and co-head instructor and openly deferred to his judgment in all things.

We have learned that at the level of white belt in many – if not most – martial arts programs, the enrollment of females and males is about even, but as students progress in rank there are fewer and fewer girls and women left in the class. Even though women and girls are no longer legally prohibited from training in mixed-sex schools, they infrequently find spaces that are supportive of them.

Emotional Power

With few exceptions, women come to martial arts because they fear violence. Many have already experienced violence and need to feel safe. Women already suffer disproportionately from low self-esteem, and this problem is only exacerbated by the frequency of violence against them. Because romance in our culture is based on power and domination, many women are attracted to powerful men, such as a black belt. These facts leave women particularly vulnerable to abuse in the dojang, especially if their instructor is a skilled rescuer.

White belts are often in awe of black belts. At white belt it's hard to imagine yourself having so much control of your body. Most white belts really don't believe they can ever be a black belt. Black belts seem magical! The veneration surrounding the black belt has led to many cultlike martial arts styles and schools. These are the schools where no one questions the master's instructions, no matter how abusive he is. Instead of a mutual respect between teacher and student, the student is the disciple of the instructor.

When Laura started martial arts, her instructor was in the hospital for an extended period of time. Everyone referred to him as "Master," with a tone of reverence and respect she had never before experienced. She was terrified to meet him. She wanted so much for him to be impressed with her that she visited him with her first broken board in hand as a gift. Now it seems ridiculous! How many broken boards this man has seen! But he was extraordinarily gracious and Laura continued to be in awe of him for many years. During the years she trained with him, even after given permission, she refused to call him by his first name because it felt disrespectful.

One of Jennifer's colleagues contacted her with a request for help. She had been training in Karate. Her instructor had manipulated her into a sexual relationship, and when she attempted to end it, he humiliated her by disparaging her in front of her fellow students, many of whom she considered friends (calling her names and criticizing her viciously as a martial artist and as a woman). Sadly, these "friends" withdrew their support from her and maintained an allegiance to the instructor. Not only did she feel exploited by the instructor, but she lost an important part of her life (training in Karate) and suffered the immediate loss of her support network, which had consisted almost entirely of other martial artists. It took her several years to recover from the emotional devastation of that experience.

In another case, a woman who had read one of Jennifer's books contacted her with a concern. She and her son were taking Karate lessons from a young instructor whom the boy looked up to. The woman was concerned because the instructor often made sexist comments about the women in class. He also made inaccurate and hurtful remarks about women's abilities. The woman wanted to address this but was afraid it would lead to repercussions against her son, who greatly enjoyed his training and did not want to switch schools. Jennifer asked her to consider what the instructor was teaching her son. For her to stand by and let that happen was unacceptable (at least in Jennifer's view). The woman later reported that she had mustered the courage to confront the instructor about his attitudes, and that the situation had improved. She further reported that it had also given her the opportunity to discuss sexist attitudes with her son.

Power dynamics are complicated and difficult to address. As instructors, it is our job to be vigilantly aware of the various kinds of power relationships that exist in our schools, and to design an atmosphere and a curriculum that encourage the empowerment of the disadvantaged and discourage the misuse of power. When thinking about your female students, it's important to remember that women grow up being told they are weaker and slower than men. In many women's minds, men are the fighters and women are the caregivers. So not only may a woman not see herself as a black belt, she also may not be able to see herself ever performing as well as a man.

CHAPTER FOUR: HIERARCHIES AND RANK

Earning a black belt is often considered the ultimate achievement in martial arts. But what is a black belt? In short, a black belt is a designation of rank, and rank is a designation of status within a formal hierarchy. To put it another way, rank is the relative position of things or persons in a group. A hierarchy is some structural organization consisting of two or more positions of unequal rank. Because rank implies power and deference, it's important to think about what it means in relationship to martial arts, in general, and for women training in martial arts in particular. This chapter focuses on ranking structures and their impact on women martial artists.

Almost all human activities are organized into some form of hierarchy. Some of them are plainly visible, while others are more subtle or even invisible. Today the majority of martial arts have some form of explicit ranking system. In fact some form of hierarchical structure is inherent in all traditional martial arts. A wide range of ranking systems have been developed, from the basic instructor-student relationship, to extremely elaborate systems that sometimes including several intermediary steps between each belt color.

Martial arts ranking structures are typically spelled out with little ambiguity. Obviously the rules and requirements underlying these systems include time and curriculum requirements. But in addition, rank almost always brings with it privileges that have little or nothing to do with personal achievement.

For example, both of us learned (in different dojangs!) that no underling was to adjust her uniform or belt while facing a black belt. This is a purely deferential requirement based on the belt color of others in the dojang. This kind of hierarchical discipline is often lauded as one of the primary benefits of martial arts training.

Ranking structures are as diverse and numerous as styles and schools. Some schools have only two or three ranks, while others have many intermediate steps making up a dozen or more ranks. Some systems have several degrees of black belt, while others stop all rank promotions at black belt.

Traditional Tae Kwon Do schools, for example, have nine student ranks. This decision was made because the numbers three and nine have enormous significance in Korean culture. Moreover, each belt color has been assigned meaning. For example, white signifies a birth, or beginning, of a seed, while green signifies the "plant" (i.e., the student) growing in knowledge and understanding of the art. There are also nine degrees of black belt in many traditional Tae Kwon Do schools.

There are many stories about how the first martial arts ranking systems developed. One of the most popular (and romantic) is the myth that a black belt was a student's white belt that had gotten so dirty from training that it turned black. While this story is inspiring, it has no basis in fact. However, it is true that middle ranks are a relatively recent addition to martial arts training systems. Several styles of martial arts claim to be the originators of the colored or "in between" belt ranks. It's likely that the first middle rank was introduced as a way of organizing class curriculum and tournament competition. In fact most instructors will tell you that rank is primarily a tool for quickly identifying students' training levels. But for whatever reason, having any ranking system in martial arts at all is paradoxical.

The Paradox of Rank

One of the goals of training in a martial art is "focus," or learning to stay in the moment. This is usually understood ideologically or psychologically, but is also a pragmatic matter. For example, if we find ourselves in a confrontational or violent situation, the last thing we need to be doing is worrying about the groceries we forgot to get after work or the report that's due in class tomorrow. We need to focus, to be completely present in the moment.

It is ironic, then, that martial arts, which are historically bound with Eastern cultures and Buddhism, urge us to think continuously about our next rank testing and to achieve that next belt color. Buddhist monk and scholar Thich Nhat Hanh said, "The destination is not the purpose of a journey. Death is not the purpose of life." If we are continually looking ahead, we end up missing all that is here now. We can't count the number of times we've heard new students say that their whole aim in martial arts training is to earn a black belt. We always want to pause and ask them, "Why?" What does a black belt mean? Better yet, what does it mean to be a black belt?

One of our biggest pet peeves as instructors is the question, "Will I need to know that for the test?" While providing tangible goals, ranking structures discourage students from embracing their journey for its own sake. As students progress in martial arts, hopefully they come to understand that rank shouldn't be the primary goal of training. Rank is simply a mile marker along the journey. We tell our students to enjoy training! When you're a white belt, *be* a white belt. When you're a green belt, *be* a green belt. Then, when you're a black belt, you'll be able to look back on your journey without disappointment or regret.

It is essential to remember that the process of learning to embrace one's journey over and above one's goals is part of the process of the martial arts journey itself. It's important for instructors to have patience with students seeking rank and recognition. At the same time, it's up to instructors to help students recognize the paradox of rank.

Rank means different things to different people, but that doesn't mean that the essence of rank is relative. Recognition for our achievements based on legitimate standards is important, especially for girls and women. Standards vary widely from art to art, system to system, and school to school. But most legitimate martial arts instructors would agree that each student progresses differently along a path of objective standards and that she should be judged according to her own unique strengths and weaknesses. Ultimately rank is a sign of a student's trust in her instructor and her art's traditions.

Training Women in the Martial Arts

The process of growth and achievement found in martial arts training is similar to that found in almost any kind of practice. The difference is that formal ranking systems provide standards, mile markers and official recognition enabling a more conscious sense of self-improvement in participants. Thus rank distinguishes martial arts from most other sports and activities.

Before Laura opened her dojang, she wrestled long and hard with the question of whether or not to have a ranking system. She felt that women learn enough deference in their lives and that the last thing martial arts training should do is to validate or extend deference for women. Martial arts training is supposed to be about empowerment. Yet ranking structures encourage, and in fact require, deference. It seems contradictory to require deference to become empowered. Perhaps it is. But empowerment also requires the recognition of achievement, such that rank provides. Laura wondered if having a ranking structure would hinder students from gaining self-approval and authority.

Jennifer wrestled with this same question when she had to decide whether to continue her dan testing. After she received her second dan, she began to believe that the testing and the promotions were no longer measuring anything about her growth in martial arts. She decided that she could be the one to decide whether she was continuing to learn and grow in her training – she did not need an outsider to put his stamp of approval on her.

Jennifer focuses on training students in seminars, lectures and workshops around the country and doesn't own a school, so she is not in a position to train and motivate the same students day after day. Because of this, she has no need to concentrate on rank in her training sessions, except to recognize it when she guest instructs at another's school. Openly acknowledging her status has both benefits and drawbacks. Because Jennifer does not stress rank during her seminars, her students aren't expected to defer to her in any formal way. At the same time, it is Jennifer's rank that designates her authority as an instructor, so her students still tend to defer to her as a superior.

Because she has trained in and taught Tae Kwon Do, Jennifer knows that rank recognition certainly helps with encouraging and motivating students day after day, week after week in their training. Laura agrees. She appreciates that her students need progress markers to help them along their journey. But she becomes discouraged when her students show more interest in receiving their next belt than in becoming more proficient at their art. She believes that testing promotes this sort of mindset. But because her school is part of a larger organization, she is obligated to continue testing. And even though Laura feels that she no longer needs outside validation for a sense of self-worth, she has noticed that an impending dan testing will induce her to train a bit harder.

Although formal ranking systems are most often associated with martial arts, other sports and activities have hierarchical structures. Along with martial arts training Laura is an avid mountain biker. For some time, she was a professionally sponsored competitive racer and was doing pretty well. Racers fall into a ranking structure where the winners are ranked higher than the losers. Laura began to feel that the need to win was impeding her self-growth rather than encouraging it. Instead of enjoying the ride she found herself worrying about how fast she could climb and descend the hill. She spent more time looking at her odometer than the beautiful trails around her. She has since removed the computers from her bikes.

In the same way, Jennifer faced considerable competition when she decided to make a living as a writer. To earn money, she had to be published. To be published, she had to push constantly to find commercial, marketable subjects to write about and to write about subjects in ways that would appeal to a mass consumer market. Jennifer was successful in this but found that she was no longer enjoying writing for the sake of writing, for the beauty of the language and the opportunity to tell a story. Instead, she was writing the way you work at McDonald's – to pay the rent. Her focus had become grinding out one article or book after another. So she made a conscious decision to step back from that goal-oriented approach and become more process-oriented. She had always enjoyed writing fiction but had never had much time for it. She decided to make the time. Now she works on her craft for a few hours every day, even though the stories and novels she writes might never be published or might not ever earn her a penny. She realized that just focusing on the next sale had derailed her from appreciating the fact that she was making a living by doing something she loved.

We both realized that focusing on the next rank encouraged us to miss the beauty of our martial arts journey. But just as an upcoming dan test motivates Laura to train harder, so will an upcoming mountain biking vacation. And having to make a rent payment will keep Jennifer planted at the computer until she's inspired to say something. Setting personal goals can be a wonderful source of inspiration. Laura has come to believe that this aspect of formal hierarchy offers an invaluable experience for students. Jennifer agrees – but because she is not awarding belts and dan levels as an instructor, she has the luxury of no longer pursuing them herself.

We should never dismiss the value of goal setting or standards. But when we become dependent on external reward we risk becoming more concerned with how others view us than how we view ourselves – a sure sign of poor self-esteem.

Laura once had a twelve-year-old student who had serious self-esteem issues. She had a poor attitude and was fixated on others' opinions of her and on achieving the next rank. During a regular class, in which she was performing more poorly than usual, she blithely informed Laura that she had mastered her technique enough that she should be awarded a black belt. Laura decided to test the student's conviction and offered her a black belt that Laura had in the school. The student took the belt and backed away. After some consideration she refused to put it on, realizing that a black belt is more than a status symbol – it is earned through work and skill mastery.

Women and Hierarchy

Because martial arts incorporate strict ranking codes, it's easy to suppose that there is no room for other hierarchies in the dojang. But even if an individual achieves a high-ranking position in one hierarchy, her position in other hierarchies does not necessarily change. To put it another way, the ranking structures that exist outside the dojang don't simply disappear when one bows in for class.

As women we are members of a low-ranking social group. Even though we make up the majority of humans on this planet, we are still considered a "minority" group. We are denied promotion, power and status both inside and outside the dojang, based solely on our sex. The codes of patriarchal society dictate that we behave in certain ways in the presence of certain people. In particular, there are strict behavioral norms for women in relationship to men. These norms affect how we interact with them, outside and inside the training hall. These codes also deeply affect how we view ourselves and our capabilities in comparison with men's.

Women have been denied access to all sorts of institutions of learning. In some places in the world, women are still denied a basic education. It is vitally important that women continue to struggle to gain access to these institutions and to earn the markers of success that they employ. This kind of affirmative action helps to narrow the power gap between men and women. Every woman who earns a black belt is an inspiration for all those who aspire to it.

Women have been warriors throughout the ages. Even so, there are only a few examples of women-specific martial arts, such as naginata (a stick-fighting martial art that uses a long weapon resembling a halberd). Most martial arts are practiced today were developed as a means of military hand-to-hand combat training, which means they were almost exclusively developed for men for the purpose of fighting with "enemies" who were strangers. Tae Kwon Do, for example, was originally developed as a method of hand-to-hand fighting for the

Korean military. So in general, martial arts have certain qualitative features that disregard women altogether.

Naturally, civilian martial arts continued to be male-oriented and dominated. In fact, until the rise of the women's movement in the 1970s, women were openly forbidden from training. But even though women have won the legal right to train, the struggle is far from over. Volumes of personal experiences from women martial artists who had to (and continue to) fight their way into the dojang, and fight to stay there and be treated with respect, refute the claim that sexism is no longer prevalent in the training hall. What almost all men fail to recognize is that sexist hierarchies are so ubiquitous that even with the best intentions, men often unconsciously act in ways that undermine women's autonomy and self-reliance.

It is unfortunate, but true, that in this society both obvious and subtle forms of sexism are inescapable in any mixed-sex framework. Women and girls are still very strongly discouraged from training, either by being physically bullied from the training hall or by being ostracized as being unfeminine – both inside and outside the dojang. We've both had more than one student confide in us that she would no longer be coming to class because her boyfriend forbade it. Over the years many of our Tae Kwon Do students have been forced to quit training because of pressures from husbands or boyfriends. A woman taking fitness kickboxing is even intimidating to some men! After teaching a session of CardioKicks! at a local gym a young woman told Laura that even though she loved the class, and in fact felt powerful for the first time in her life, she would no longer be attending because her boyfriend wasn't happy about it.

Jennifer's parents constantly pressured her to quit training over concerns about her getting hurt fighting men, despite the obvious safety factors (safety gear, low contact, strict rules regarding sparring less-skilled opponents). They also frequently expressed doubt that she would ever be able to use what she had learned in a self-defense situation because, of course, men were bigger and stronger than women – so what was the point?

If she had been younger or more dependent on them, the pressure could easily have caused her to quit her training early on.

In another illuminating experience, a boyfriend broke up with Jennifer because her expertise in martial arts made him feel threatened. "Who was the man in the relationship?" he wanted to know. In both instances Jennifer was stepping outside of prescribed gender roles and this caused a lot of anxiety for those close to her. Their responses reveal how deeply engrained these attitudes run. Jennifer's parents minimized the value of her training while expressing concern for her safety, while her boyfriend tried to make her feel unfeminine because of her training. These kinds of pressures often result in female students quitting. It's important that instructors recognize and discuss these common reactions with their students.

Hidden Hierarchies

Many martial arts instructors and students believe that when they step into a training hall, the objective relationship of social power that exists between men and women somehow doesn't apply to them. In fact, this relationship is often more deeply obscured behind the constructs of the overt hierarchy. No amount of good intention alone will make a dojang immune from this dynamic.

For both of us, one of the privileges of being a black belt in the dojangs where we first trained was to be addressed by title and surname, e.g. Miss, Mrs., or Mr. Smith. (Or Master after some degree of black belt.) Both of us created quite a stir in our schools when we became black belts because we wanted to be called "Ms." We had both kept our birth names when we married our husbands, so it was the correct designation. Both of us were surprised to find that this was not comfortable for many of our fellow black belts. Laura was confronted by a female second-degree black belt who just couldn't understand why she didn't consider her marital status pertinent to her training. Laura tried to explain to her that she was not married to her father, but her fellow student still refused to call her Ms. Kamienski.

When an individual or group that is lower in a hierarchy challenges the authority of the dominant group, she is often met with strong resistance. Over the years Laura has met with a number of men who feel threatened enough by her women-only studio to contact her. One in particular (mentioned in the Introduction), a fellow black belt in Tae Kwon Do, accused her of "stripping Tae Kwon Do of its true meaning" by excluding men and boys. Never mind his arrogance or the fact that women have been excluded from Tae Kwon Do training for a good bit of its history; the fact that this man felt compelled to criticize Laura's dojang was the result of her challenging his position on the totem pole.

Those on top of any hierarchy naturally become the standard measure for all members. One of the ways this is expressed in our culture is through the use of the term "men" to refer to all people, and the default use of the pronoun "he" when the sex of an individual is unknown.

When Jennifer wrote a book about the principles of martial arts, a bookseller who practiced Karate confronted her and demanded to know why she didn't "warn" readers that the book was for women. He even suggested a disclaimer on the front! Two things were of interest about his distress: The first was that the cover did, in fact, include an illustration of a woman doing a technique – the only illustration present on the cover, so it was hard to miss. The second was that the information presented in the book was not in any way exclusive to women; Jennifer just used female examples and the female pronoun equally with the male. But this was considered an affront to a person who assumed that "male" was the standard martial artist and that readers had to be warned if she was also going to be talking about women.

Since opening her womens-only martial arts studio, Laura has experienced a many types of sexism and sexist violence ranging from physical threats, personal insults and accusations of being a "man-hater," to arrogant dismissals of doing anything of value. She has heard reports of friends of students whose male partners won't permit them to train at Kicks. The power that these men wield over their partners reveals how deeply men affect women's ability to self-govern.

We have both seen many female students quit their training because of pressure about spending too much time away from home duties or because of being labeled as "one of those feminists, a lesbian, or a man-hater." And both of us have received dozens of e-mails, letters and phone calls from men who are challenged by the work that we do.

One example came from a man named Johnny who said, "Women like you are dangerous. They are a real threat to our male superiority. Stop showing women how to kick hard and low, stop it. It's not fair."

And Thomas wrote, "I read a brief bio of you today on a self-defense web site and you are impressive! I was captivated when I read that you knew how to wrestle. I would love to wrestle with you one day. I would like for you to kick and stomp me in the groin as we wrestled. Would it be possible to arrange a private wrestling match with you one day?"

And Mike wrote, "What do you think about groin kicks as self-defense move? Do you think it is a good move for a non-martial expert? And in real life, have you ever used this technique to defend yourself in a dangerous situation? Do [you] happen to kick or knee guys in the groin during sparring? I don't mean because you [meant to but what if] you made a 'terrible mistake' and got them or maybe you did it because you wished to do it? If yes, may you describe the situation to me?"

Recently Laura received a phone call from a man who claimed his wife had taken a self-defense course with her. He proceeded to describe how his wife had kneed and kicked him in the groin causing swollen testicles, which he felt compelled to describe in some detail.

And as a final example, Edwin wrote: "I am a man and I want to learn karate, however, most all men are physically and mentally more aggressive and superior than me. So I thought it would be a good idea to start out in a women's class or something…."

Training Women in the Martial Arts

Though extreme, this type of thinking is carried over to what is often considered legitimate criticism of women's programs. The most common disparagement claims that women's classes are fine at the introductory level, suggesting that advanced training without men is inferior. This attack alleges that men are naturally better, more aggressive fighters and that providing "comfort in a foreign environment" is the only benefit of women-only training. While this provision is indeed fortuitous, the argument fails to recognize more significant advantages such as the opportunity for women to experience autonomy, control and positions of authority and leadership, uninhibited by male dominance.

One of the most revealing responses was an incident that took place after a self-defense workshop. One of the women who took the class returned to the studio with her husband. He entered the studio with a huge chip on his shoulder; his wife shrank back just outside the door. Laura's co-instructor greeted him and asked what she could do for him. He told her that he wanted to check out the place and see where his wife had just been training. He proceeded to look around and finally said, "I really just wanted to tell you that the choke defense you taught my wife doesn't work. She tried it on me and it doesn't work." Laura's co-instructor, realizing that he was trying to pick a fight with her, very calmly and assertively replied that it didn't work because his wife wasn't willing to hurt him. The man got the message and left quietly.

Since we've started training, we can't count the number of times that we've been in public while wearing a martial arts T-shirt or jacket and a man taunts us with a comment like, "Oh, I'm not going to mess with you!" Laura always replies with a sarcastically coy "Thank you. But would you mess with me if I didn't practice martial arts?" She's most often met with a "Hmm" followed by a thoughtful stare.

One time a young man noticed Laura's T-shirt and they had their exchange. He thought for a moment and quite frankly said, "Yep, ya know what, I probably would." His honesty was refreshing! His deep-seated sense of entitlement is pervasive among men living in a sexist culture. What becomes clear when looking at these types of responses to women's training is that women are expected to stay in their place; a place that doesn't include training in a martial art or learning self-defense.

Authority in the Training Hall

Women control and head very few martial arts studios. Those studios that have a female head tend to be either exclusively for women or have a student base that is overwhelmingly female. It's a fact that most people don't take female martial artists as seriously as male martial artists. It's difficult for women to gain authority in any setting let alone a setting that has been dominated by men for centuries.

There are studios that have women in leadership positions, but they are almost always second or third in the command chain and are often responsible for traditionally female tasks such as teaching children and bookkeeping. Jennifer recalls one school run by a female head who employed male instructors to teach most of the classes so that she could attract male students to the school. She had also bought into many of the sexist myths and misconceptions about women in martial arts that male school owners usually do. Laura has often been criticized, by both women and men, for teaching "weaker" or "softer" martial arts than her male counterparts, making it more difficult for her to gain legitimacy as an instructor. Sexist attitudes run so deep that many times it isn't men, but women who subscribe to and perpetuate them.

It's not surprising that the same male dominance holds true for most of the larger martial arts organizations that we've reviewed. At a recent convention of one of the largest martial arts professional organizations in the United States, only six instructors out of about 50 were women. Further, those women who were contracted to teach were overwhelmingly teaching courses on "little ninja" or children's programs, fitness, yoga, and promoting martial arts to women. This was hardly an equal distribution of responsibility the organization claimed to have. And except for a financial officer (administrative), all of the officers of the organization were male.

Laura will never forget the moment she realized that she could, and in fact had to, make decisions regarding the curriculum at her school. It was one of the most liberating moments of her life. Until then she had relied on and yielded to the dictates and opinions of her superiors — all men. The moment she made her first autonomous decision, she realized she was an authority and had authority. Until then her black belt had just been something that had been given to her. She had no idea whether she really was a black belt. She was taking someone else's word for it. Afterward she knew she had earned it and that it was a part of her.

When Jennifer was teaching a women-only self-defense class at a woman-owned mixed sex martial arts school, a male instructor barged into the training and tried to interfere with the instruction. Jennifer had been working with the women on their kihaps (shout), having them practice saying what they wanted with a straight face, no smiles, no laughing (i.e., "Leave me alone," or "I don't want you to do that."). This instructor immediately began telling the women that there was a time

Special Needs

Women and girls with special needs are particularly vulnerable to violence. They may have physical, cognitive or emotional challenges that not only make them more vulnerable to violence, but also may make it more difficult for them to resist violence. Accommodations can be made to help them modify the techniques if a physical challenge, for example, prevents them from doing the technique as it is usually done. But more importantly, these women and girls need to be able to understand the tools and resources available to them to prevent and solve violence in their lives. By working with them individually, instructors can learn how to help them become the best martial artists possible, and to help them devise strategies and tactics appropriate to their personal situations.

and place for yelling, and that they should tone down their responses if they were uncomfortable expressing themselves or if they were with men they knew – which defeated the whole purpose of the exercise. After all, learning to be assertive toward a potential attacker was the main goal of the exercise. Since attackers are almost always men whom women know, it makes no sense to "tone down their responses" toward them. Jennifer asked him to leave because of the disruption of the training dynamic he caused and his immediate usurpation of authority.

Whether or not there is a formal ranking structure at a studio, instructors must become aware of pre-existing hierarchies and the way the dynamics of these hierarchies affect both women's and men's training. Depending on the situation, it may make sense to incorporate formal rules regarding sexist (or racist or homophobic) behavior and strictly enforce them. Though in and of themselves, these rules won't solve the problem, they will set a standard for the kind of treatment female students should expect.

What You Can Do to Support Female Martial Artists

This section has discussed some of the hurdles women face to begin training, the resistance they meet while training, and the difficulties they encounter as instructors. It's important for instructors, co-students and supporters alike to be aware of pre-existing hierarchies and gendered behavior, and to be willing to provide for the special needs of female students. In doing so, we must be willing to openly condemn any behavior that inhibits, discourages or obstructs a student's training. This includes behaviors that might not seem inappropriate (and might even seem kind!) but nonetheless result in perpetuating sexist attitudes, which undermine women martial artists.

CHAPTER FIVE: FORGING NEW TRADITIONS

Laura remembers the decision to leave her original dojang and instructor as being one of the most difficult and heart-wrenching choices she has ever had to make. Her instructor was one of her closest friends and many of the students she trained with were like family. But as Laura began to uncover the truth about violence against women and the ways in which her training was lacking, she eventually found that she needed to break out on her own in order to develop as a martial artist and an instructor.

One of the first experiences that led Laura to this decision was when she organized a women's self-defense seminar at a local women's fitness studio. She was to co-teach the course with her instructor according to the pre-established curriculum of a combative-style course. Laura's recent domestic violence advocacy training made her realize the necessity for time and space to practice other skills and to safely share experiences. She approached her instructor and asked his permission to have a couple of sessions with the students to work on other types of skills. This was fine with him until she suggested that he not be present. He flatly refused! For the first time Laura did not "obey" him. She felt strongly enough about her conviction to continue the debate. Eventually her instructor offered her a compromise. He told her that he wouldn't change the existing course, but would add one more session so that she "could have [her] *little girl* time." Even though Laura had heard sexist remarks from her instructor in the past, this was the first time she felt confident enough in her own authority as an instructor to stand up to him. This confrontation was the beginning of the end of their association. It took a long time for Laura to recover from the loss of her former instructor and dojang, but she now feels no regret. In fact, Laura knows that she would not be the person she is today had she not found the courage and conviction to step out on her own.

Despite feeling strongly that her instructor contributed directly to her personal growth, Jennifer eventually disengaged from her original school because she felt she could learn more and offer more being on her own. Like Laura, she began to discover more about violence against women and wanted to use her skills to help end such violence.

As part of a demo team, Jennifer often went with her instructor to give workshops. One day she was discussing with the demo group the curriculum for a self-defense class to be taught at a local sorority. The instructor discussed various self-defense strategies they would demonstrate. Jennifer brought up the point that many young women are raped by men they know, and that the group should consider strategies they could teach to women who knew their attackers. The instructor abruptly cut off thr conversation and said, "They shouldn't be in that situation in the first place." Jennifer was shocked by this response. She declined to participate in the demo and began the process of going out on her own.

Our responses are now part of a long history of feminist responses to male-dominated martial arts. Kicks Martial Arts for Women is one of dozens of women-only martial arts studios throughout the world.

Kicks Martial Arts for Women: Forging New Traditions

We've already mentioned some of the new traditions that Laura has established at her dojang, such as setting boundaries before every contact drill. Before opening Kicks, Laura also spent a lot of time deciding what kind of uniform to use. She found that wearing the traditional wrap-type Japanese gi style of uniform was restrictive. She often preferred to wear just a sports bra under her jacket when training and found that the gi top would open up during intense workouts. So she decided to use a V-neck uniform instead. She also noticed that some women came to class wearing make-up and that by the end of class they would have orange collars. With this in mind, she felt that black collars would be useful even though they were traditionally only worn by WTF black belts. Finally she decided that black pants would be practical for women during menstruation, so black pants became a permissible part of the Kicks' dobok.

The traditional Tae Kwon Do student oath includes a promise to respect one's instructors and seniors. Laura decided to add "and fellow students" to this line in an attempt to break down artificial deference and hierarchical norms. Not only does she feel that each student deserves to be respected in her own right, but that there are plenty of black belts out there who deserve little respect. Respect should be a choice, not a requirement. It must be earned, not demanded.

To encourage creativity and confidence in their own authority, Kicks' students are required to choreograph their own form before testing for red/black belt. This requirement not only promotes self-esteem in each student, but adds to the overall self-determination of the dojang.

Another new tradition at Kicks is an annual fundraiser called Kick Back Against Violence, which is held to raise money for a local women's shelter and community center. Students ask friends and family to sign their names and pledge an amount on a pine board which they will in turn break. It has been an amazingly successful campaign and a lot of fun for everyone involved.

One of the most valued new traditions at Kicks is a public speaking assignment. At blue belt students are asked to give a five- to ten-minute presentation on what their training means to them. Over the years these presentations have taken many forms, including musical and poetic. But invariably they have deepened the sense of connection between students at Kicks, who have remarked that hearing others speak about their own training helps them to feel less alone and to understand that they share many of the same fears and triumphs. Many students have chosen to disclose their own experiences with violence during their presentations.

A History of New Traditions

The development of schools and organizations for women martial artists is a significant part of women's efforts to forge their own new traditions. For example, the National Women's Martial Arts Federation (NWMAF) and the Pacific Association of Women Martial Artists (PAWMA) are organizations whose mission is to promote the involvement of women and girls in the martial arts. The NWMAF holds an annual training camp called "Special Training" where women martial artists of many different styles and from all over the world come together to train for one intense weekend.

Laura's first Special Training was a huge eye opener. Being in the company of hundreds of extraordinarily accomplished women who were in control not only of their bodies, but of their training and their schools, was incredible. On the final evening of each Special Training, a demonstration consisting entirely of women is presented. This demonstration changed Laura's view of martial arts entirely. For the first time she actually believed in her own power. When she returned home she watched a rerun of the movie *Roadhouse*. Fight scenes which had once looked powerful now looked amiss because they didn't include women, and in fact the movie pictured women in the background responding in completely ineffectual gendered ways. Laura now requires her students to attend at least one Special Training before testing for black belt. She feels that the experience is invaluable for her students.

The NWMAF also offers self-defense instructor certification. This certification is comprehensive and includes preparing instructors to teach both physical and nonphysical defense skills. Unlike other self-defense certifications, NWMAF instructor certification is based on promoting a philosophy of women's empowerment and social justice.

Working alongside the NWMAF and PAWMA is the Association of Women Martial Arts Instructors, organized by a group of professional female martial artists for the purpose of catching those women martial artists who had fallen through the cracks of the male martial arts world and to provide them with options for rank and recognition. When Laura was forced to leave her original school because of disagreements about the role of women in the training hall, the AWMAI was a welcomed resource.

The fact that these and other organizations like them exist reveals that the social and political oppression of women plays a significant role in the violence we experience, and that this must be reflected in our martial arts training. However, some of those working in the anti-violence movement today consider violence against women a personal issue first and a political issue only secondarily. Others recognize violence against women as a political issue, but narrowly define rape and battering as isolated phenomena, disconnected from larger issues of oppression and violence. This tendency is part of a retreat by the women's movement. It is a result of reactionary backlash and ongoing attacks that threaten the gains made by feminists throughout history.

Oppression serves a specific group of people by dividing and weakening those who are struggling for equality. Every form of oppression has a corresponding form of violence. Violence against women is a systematic and structural method of maintaining the oppression of women through rape, domestic violence, and many other less aggressive forms of harassment, such as cat-calls, demeaning and devaluing language, and mediated objectification. Oppression is part of how a privileged group rules. It is a part of the superstructure of society. From this perspective, ideas like racism, sexism, anti-gay bigotry, national chauvinism, religious chauvinism, etc., are all examples of how the status quo articulates its ideological hegemony over society as a whole.

To the extent that economic issues and children have an impact on a battered woman's strategy for escape, affirmative action and reproductive rights are directly related and central to the struggle, yet many women's organizations refuse to even consider discussing the issue of abortion or affirmative action. What battered women need — access to affordable housing, living-wage jobs, free and accessible child care (not that much different from what all women need to lead independent lives) — is not something that will be obtained by either providing shelter services or arresting batterers. Individualizing, personalizing or reducing the issue of sexist violence to gender roles and safe dating practices isn't going to end battering or rape, which are (and always have been) tools of systematic sexism. And since not all survivors are white or middle class, rape and battering are also (as they always have been) issues of racism and economic inequality. The history of the Battered Women's Shelter Movement is deeply and necessarily conjoined with the women's liberation movement, as is all self-defense and anti-violence work.

Laura tells her students that Kicks is the "Sears" of self-defense. Kicks offers a wide selection of tools and materials, but how, what and where students choose to build will ultimately be up to them. Laura reminds her students that she probably won't be there should they be attacked, so they will need to assess the situation and devise strategies for themselves. Critical thinking skills are essential for effective self-defense. Being able to break cement blocks is simply a tool. If we don't learn how to design our projects effectively, our tools are rendered useless.

What's more is that you may not have a hammer available when you need one, so you'll need to improvise. There is only one unalterable self-defense "tip" that we offer our students, and that is to think about what they can do and not about what they can't do. After all, there is absolutely no self-defense technique that will work in every situation, but—unless you're dead—there is no situation in which there isn't *something* you can do to improve your chances for safety.

Who Should Teach?

Now we come to the question of who should be teaching women self-defense. There are many reasons why women should be the primary instructor or coach in a women's self defense class. (Notice we did not say co-sex self-defense class.) Evidence suggests that women who come to a women's self-defense class come because they feel more comfortable there. They will be more likely to talk about what they need to gain from the course. But more important is the fact that men simply cannot intuitively understand the socialization process that women undergo. Gavin De Becker put it well when he said, "Men are afraid that women will laugh at them. Women are afraid that men will kill them." It is nearly impossible for men to understand how deeply women fear them. It is this very understanding that can best help women to learn self defense. All the techniques in the world won't help you if you're not willing or able to use them.

Many male instructors claim that they are as capable, if not more, of teaching women self-defense. While there are many male self-defense instructors out there who are competent at teaching physical technique, teaching women to get free from a wrist grab or "street fighting" techniques is only a small portion of teaching women self-defense. Women must first value themselves enough to want to defend themselves; then they must somehow come to believe they actually can. Some women have accomplished this. For them, a nonfeminist self-defense course that focuses exclusively on learning physical technique might have more value. But for a huge number of women, learning about and understanding the socialization process is pivotal for learning self-defense. Men simply don't need to think about the effects of socialization when learning to fight. They have been trained to be independent, autonomous and to fight from the moment of their birth. This is not true for women.

Women who train in martial arts are intimately familiar with traditional models of instruction. On the other hand, male martial artists are sorely unfamiliar with what women need for successful training. As we have repeatedly mentioned throughout this book, traditional training is universally based on myths of stranger danger, and fall short of providing opportunities for women to learn skills to defend themselves before an assault turns physically aggressive. Offering statistics or simply mentioning acquaintance rape is only giving lip-service to "prevention."

Women-Only Spaces: Our Own Tradition

It is encouraging that many martial arts schools are incorporating women-only classes as part of their regular offerings. At the very least, this trend represents an acknowledgment that women have special training needs. However, it's important to remember that these classes need to be appropriately focused. In addition, women's classes should never be considered or described as secondary or inferior to co-sex classes in any way. It is vitally important that women-only classes be actively promoted as an integral part of the female student's training. Representing women's classes as ineffective or secondary is not only bogus, it is extremely damaging for women martial artists.

There are several common assumptions behind the idea that women's classes are inferior. The first is that training with men is somehow more intense than training without them. Many people believe that men must be involved in women's self-defense because "human nature" leaves women in vulnerable positions. The editor of one martial arts trade magazine openly claimed that women are only capable of teaching "pooh bear" self-defense. Training without men is criticized as inadequate because the violence committed against women is usually committed by men. It is true that violence against women is overwhelmingly committed by men, but to say that women must train with men in order to experience a mock assault implies that men are naturally better, more aggressive fighters.

We have learned that not only is this assumption sexist but is simply false. In all of our experience training in women-only classes, the overall intensity level is not only equal to but in some instances is greater than in mixed sex settings. Fighting a female attacker/training partner proved no less intense or inferior to fighting a male attacker/training partner in any way. Moreover, any course that claims to have "realistic" full contact training is one to be wary of. To be truly realistic there must be a possibility to complete a rape or murder. There are no legitimate courses that don't have at least minimal safety protocols.

Another common assumption is that training with men is universally more empowering for women. For some women it is empowering to fight against a male opponent. But whatever the psychological benefit of this aspect of training, the fact remains that it is perceived as beneficial based on perceptions which are both accurate and inaccurate. The reality is that violence against women is overwhelmingly committed by men. But the desire to train against a male opponent is also based on misinformation about male-female size disparity and on the sexist notion that women are incapable of fighting as proficiently and effectively as men. This assumption also neglects to account for the many women who find training with men to be disempowering. Their experience is one riddled with diminutive remarks, demeaning behavior and attempts to undermine and control autonomy and self-determination.

A third assumption is that women's spaces are fine for "introductory classes" only. This implies that advanced training without men is inferior in some way. This is the same kind of sexist thinking that has relegated women to secondary roles and status in many arenas. Those who assert this line allege that the only benefit for training without men is that it affords women an initial period of "comfort in a foreign environment." This is one important aspect of women's training. However, this logic fails to recognize other, more significant benefits that women's spaces provide, such as the opportunity for women to make all of their own decisions free from male dominance, to model women in leadership positions free from a male vantage point, and to explore self-defense outside of the traditional stranger-danger models. Not to mention the fact that some of the finest advanced training we've had the opportunity to participate in was in women-only classes.

Finally, some assume that since women are now training with men they are being treated equally in the training hall. As we mentioned earlier, volumes of personal experiences from women martial artists who had to (and continue to) fight their way into the dojang, to stay there, and to be treated with any kind of respect at all, refute this claim. What almost all men fail to recognize is that sexism is so ubiquitous that even with the best of intentions men often unconsciously act in ways that undermine women's autonomy and self-reliance. Because we live in a society in which women are considered second-class citizens, both overt and subtle sexism is pervasive and inescapable in any mixed-sex framework. The necessity for women-only self-defense stems from this reality.

We find it disconcerting that no one ever questions whether men were (or are) missing something when training without women. One thing that perhaps they were (and are) missing is a kind of leadership that is not only foreign to them but to which they remain resistant. The irony is that female leadership will never exist until we are afforded autonomous opportunities to develop it.

Above all other criticism, the primary objection to women-only training is that it is a form of reverse discrimination. Is providing women-only training reverse discrimination? Hardly. The point of an all-female training space is not to deprive men, but to empower women. Women who have had the opportunity to train at Kicks describe their experiences with words and phrases like: "freedom, our/my own, realizing my/our potential, not measuring myself against men, feelings of independence, confidence, power and strength as a woman and as women." All of these accounts describe autonomy. Autonomy is a prerequisite for the social and political equality of an oppressed group.

The claim of reverse discrimination implies that by endorsing women-only spaces we must then endorse men-only spaces as well, or oppose both. After all, it is argued, it was feminists who protested women's exclusion from men-only spaces; by excluding men, the women's movement is committing the same transgression. But the attempt to classify women's separatism within the same category as sexism or discrimination disregards the reality of male privilege. The exclusion of men by women and the exclusion of women by men are fundamentally different. To accuse women (or African Americans or any other disenfranchised group) of reverse discrimination is reactionary because it presumes equality between oppressor and oppressed. Because women are an oppressed group, to exclude men is not the same as men excluding women.

Accusing feminists of reverse discrimination closely resembles the reaction against the civil rights movement, which selectively used the tactic of white exclusion. At best these allegations ignore or deny the reality of existing relationships of power. At worst they are (consciously or unconsciously) racist, sexist and homophobic attacks against programs of affirmative action that feminists and other civil rights activists fought hard to win. We certainly wouldn't be so presumptuous or arrogant as privileged white women in America to assert that we are best qualified to teach self-defense to a group of African-Americans, or that courses designed specifically to address their own unique concerns and which exclude whites are somehow inferior. While we could offer them some useful skills, only African-Americans, who have experienced the violence of racism first hand, are in the best position to develop and teach effective self-defense programs for themselves.

Kicks, along with other consciously organized women-only ventures, plays a vital role in helping many women begin to recognize and analyze their oppression.

In reporting what they like about training in a women-only space, Laura's students say: "I don't have to worry about being watched," "I like it that I don't have to worry about what I look like," "I can be myself and not worry about what I say or do." These sentiments clearly indicate a sense of freedom from surveillance. Surveillance is a mechanism used to maintain subordination. As a subordinate group, women are under constant surveillance in many ways. Freedom from surveillance by the dominant group establishes an atmosphere ripe for open discussion and the development of leadership skills. Because they are free from surveillance, women at Kicks enjoy the opportunity to expand their consciousness in a less inhibiting environment. When in mixed-sex settings, women tend to react in sexually gendered ways. Men tend to intimidate most women. Even friendly supportive men have an impact on the confidence of some women.

Training Women in the Martial Arts

Throughout history feminists have incorporated women-only spaces and initiatives as a means of affirmative action. Feminism is about the empowerment of women by recognizing women's perspectives. It is not about men's perspectives at all. Women in general have different life experiences than men, and their experiences are often discounted, censured or silenced. To be a feminist is to be anti-male only in the attempt to break down what it means to be male in a society where the oppression of women is institutionalized. It means to begin to undermine how men learn to be men and women learn to be women in such a society.

If Laura had decided to open a studio that offered only children's classes, we seriously doubt that anyone would have complained that she was discriminating against adults. The problem is that Kicks threatens— deliberately so— the stability and foundations of sexism and the violence it manifests. It is a place where students can freely acknowledge that women are different from men. As a distinctly oppressed class, women train for different reasons. Women have specific self-defense needs and concerns. Women benefit from modeling themselves after female teachers and each other while not being overshadowed by men. Coming in contact with real examples of women in power has an immeasurable effect on a woman's self-image. It is the beginning of realizing her own possibilities.

Other opponents of women-only spaces claim that feminism creates and sustains women as victims in our society. This claim has a certain momentum which must be addressed. If you start from the premise that the only way to avoid bing a victim is to decide not to be one, it is easy to make the logical and practical error that women choose their role in our society deliberately and cognitively. It follows from this convoluted line of reasoning that pointing out how women become victims is not only erroneous but dangerous, and it keeps women in the role of victim. This trap is where many male (and some female) martial arts and self-defense instructors are getting caught.

While we must be careful to offer solutions with the analysis of victimization, understanding and addressing the exploitation and victimization of women is imperative in developing strategies to change that role. In other words, women as a group cannot decide to stop being victims without understanding their victimization. This is exactly why a feminist approach to teaching women's self-defense, including the incorporation of women -only classes, is absolutely key.

Uncovering gender-specific socialization should be part of any self-defense training for women. Without it, much of the training becomes useless. For example, we know many accomplished female martial artists who have been and are presently victims of sexual and physical abuse. They deal with the damage of the past and with the terror of the present on a daily basis. These women have a lot of physical skill which they've learned in the dojang and during self-defense classes. What they lack is an understanding of their own victimization. Their skills become much less valuable if not completely innocuous.

Are we confusing helping victims with teaching self-defense? We don't think so. We think that for women, they are inseparable. We are confronted with assault every day, both physical and verbal. We can't pick up a magazine or turn on the television without seeing violence against women. We can't leave our houses without experiencing some cat call or demeaning remark during the day. Most of us are taught to ignore these attacks and are even encouraged to construe them as somehow flattering; and in too many cases, we do. Verbal assault is assault! It is where most physical assaults begin for women. We need to begin self-defense training at that point.

Closing Thoughts

Reclaiming our bodies as our own is a long and difficult process. It requires unlearning and deconstructing centuries of gender training. Consciously organized women's spaces are places where women can begin to realize their own potential, free from male domination. They are places where we can begin to reclaim our bodies and our lives as our own. Claiming spaces of our own means setting new standards, forging new models and establishing new traditions. Laura is proud to say Kicks is hers, but she's even more proud to say that Kicks is *ours*.

We hope this book accomplishes several things. First, we hope it will inspire more women to train in the martial arts. Second, we hope those reading this who have a female martial artist in their lives are better prepared to continue supporting them. And finally, we hope that those who are engaged in teaching female martial artists and women's self-defense will continue to educate themselves about violence against women and incorporate the experiences of women and girls into the activities and curriculum of their courses.

Ultimately our mantra must be to seek the truth. All of our courses and activities must be based on accurate information. Any course or program for women or including women, that hasn't been developed within the context of acquaintance and intimate partner violence runs the risk of lulling them into a false sense of security, because they are much more likely to be attacked by a known, often-trusted and loved assailant than by a stranger. Courses must include activities to develop verbal boundary setting and awareness skills. This is not to say that we think that learning physical skills is useless. Learning to fight is extremely empowering and valuable. We would never discourage a woman from taking a fitness kickboxing or martial arts class. But again, it makes no sense to focus exclusively on learning combative technique. The multistrategy approach to self-defense is tried and true. The most effective courses provide physical skills, but they also provide women with opportunities to learn skills to handle the kinds of psychological manipulation and intimidation that is commonly used by perpetrators of violence.

We believe that, as a group, women are the real experts of self-defense. Women have been successfully defending themselves for centuries using many different kinds of tactics and strategies. The problem has been that our methods are usually discounted and ignored by martial arts instructors who subscribe to male models and traditions. Our greatest wish is that our voice is now being heard.

Sources and recommended reading

- Bart, Pauline B. and O'Brien, Patricia H. 1985. *Stopping Rape—Successful Survival Strategies:* Pergamon Press, NY.
- Belenky, Mary Field, Clinchy, Blythe McVicker, Goldberger, Nancy Rule and Tarule, Jill Mattuck. 1997. *Women's Ways of Knowing—The Development of Self, Voice and Mind:* Basic Books, New York, NY.
- Butler, Pamela E., Ph.D. 1992. *Self-Assertion for Women:* Harper, San Francisco, CA.
- Caignon, Denise and Groves, Gail. 1987. *Her Wits About Her—Self-Defense Success Stories by Women.* Harper & Row, New York, NY.
- Dass, Ram and Gorman, Paul. 1999. *How Can I Help?— Stories and Reflections on Service:* Alfred A. Knopf, New York, NY.
- DeBecker, Gavin. 1997. *The Gift of Fear:* Dell, New York, NY.
- DeBecker, Gavin. 1999. *Protecting the Gift:* Random House, NY.
- Evans, Patricia. 1993. *Verbal Abuse Survivors Speak Out on Relationship and Recovery:* Adams Media Corporation, Holbrook, MA.
- Grauerholz, Elizabeth and Koralewski, Mary A. 1991. *Sexual Coercion—A Sourcebook on Its Nature, Causes and Prevention:* Lexington Books, MA.
- Henley, Nancy, 1977. *Body Politics—Power Sex and Non-verbal Communication,* New York, NY.
- Langelan, Martha J. 1993. *Back Off—How to Confront and Stop Sexual Harassment and Harassers:* Fireside, New York, NY.

- McCaughey, Martha. 1997. *Real Knockouts—The Physical Feminism of Women's Self-Defense:* New York University Press, New York, NY.
- Medea, Andra and Thompson, Kathleen. 1972. *Against Rape:* Farrer, Straus and Giroux, New York, NY.
- Miller, Jean Baker, M.D. 1986. *Toward a New Psychology of Women:* Beacon Press, Boston, MA.
- Smith, Susan E. 1986. *Fear or Freedom—A Woman's Options in Social Survival & Physical Self-Defense:* Mother Courage Press, Racine, WI.
- Snortland, Ellen. 1998. *Beauty Bites Beast—Awakening the Warrior Within Women and Girls:* Trilogy, Pasadena, CA.
- Telsey, Nadia. 1988. *Self-Defense From the Inside Out— A Women's Workbook for Developing Self-Esteem and Assertiveness Skills for Safety:* Be Free, Eugene, OR.
- Tschirhart Sanford, Linda and Fetter, Ann. 1979. *In Defense of Ourselves—A Rape Prevention Handbook:* Double Day, Garden City, NY.
- Warshaw, Robin. 1994. *I Never Called It Rape:* Harper, New York, NY.
- Wiley, Carol A. 1992. *Women in the Martial Arts:* North Atlantic Books, Berkeley, CA.

APPENDIX

The following is a fictionalized presentation of a student's experience in Laura's CardioKicks! fitness kickboxing class.

Counting No's

By Taylor Chase

Ten. Eleven, even.

They stood in groups of two or three around the cheery dance floor, whispering to each other, critiquing their figures in the mirrors, eying the other girls suspiciously. Some lingered back by the doorway, shy of entering the aerobics studio until called for, while others strode right up to the front of the class. Julie surveyed the scene in the mirror behind her. In poured the girls, short shorts showing off tan legs, white T-shirts coyly revealing brightly colored sports bras, hair pulled back into long ponytails, sweat glistening off delicate necks. The room itself was sweltering; the rising temperature alone made Julie's shirt stick uncomfortably to her back and dampened the hair on her neck. The fan in the corner was set to high, but humid, stale air still hung over the entire space. Yet that didn't stop the girls from coming in, squeezing in, staking out a place on the floor where they could punch comfortably without hitting anyone else. It was hot, it was sweaty, but Thursday afternoon at five was a weekly ritual that could not be passed up. It was time for kickboxing class.

As 47, 48, 49 girls pushed in, Julie was forced up front, closer to the mirror. It didn't bother her. She could critique her movements better, not to mention keep a wary eye on any girls behind her who seemed they might lack the seriousness required of the occasion. Feet spread slightly apart, back flat as she bent down, pretending to stretch her sore right hamstring, Julie continued to count as the girls streamed in.

Fifty girls, she thought. Fifty divided by four. Twelve. Twelve and a half, really, but we'll say 12.

Twelve girls in this room have been raped.

You couldn't tell just by looking at them, she reminded her-self as she scanned the crowd. True, some of their smiles seemed a little out of place, and the brunette in the corner had an especially wary look in her eyes. But that could just be stress, school, impatience, anything. After all, she sighed, eyes and face usually don't show what a girl has been through. Occasionally you can tell. You look at a girl, and you just know. But most of the time, they get pretty good at stretching out glinting smiles and dulling in their expressions any other tell-tale signs of the past. You have to, if you want to be able to walk down the hall toward your room every day.

One in four, she repeated to herself out of habit, swinging her left leg out and stretching down. One in four women has been raped by the time she graduates from college.

The class instructor started the tape and assumed her position at the front of the room. Rachel was her name— a 120-pound, short-haired, rock-hard force that no man would ever want to mess with on a Saturday night. Half drill-sergeant, half big sister, her classes were perhaps the most regularly attended at the university. She tossed Julie a quick smile in the mirror before ordering the crowd, "Shoulders back!" One hundred arms rippled backward like a wave. With the first deep pounding of the bass, and the steady quickening of tempo, the girls behind her fell into line. In any other exercise class, they would have warmed up gradually into concentrating. But here, their muscles tensed and eyes became alert with the first floor-shaking note that resonated from the speaker. No messing around. Kickboxing was serious.

Julie began moving to the beat, barely aware of Rachel's commands continually shouted across the room. After 87 kickboxing classes she didn't really need to listen to instructions any more. She could go through the front kicks, side chops and uppercuts with the ease and rhythm of a practiced fighter, not the flurried swipes of someone trying to keep time with the music. Even after her first class, Rachel had complimented her on the already firm precision of her kicks, and how she faultlessly made impact with the heel. Julie had smiled modestly and thanked her before turning away. Precision came from training, from those nights after it happened that she spent downstairs in front of the kickboxing techniques video, playing on mute so it wouldn't wake anyone up. Side kick. Jab. Keep the arm tense and strong. Make sure it doesn't happen again. Never again.

"Five, six, seven, eight!" Rachel counted off the beats of the song, and the girls moved in unison.

First the neck, relax the neck, that's important if you want to get ready to fight. Too tight and you'll wrench a muscle. Alert, but loose enough to ebb and flow. Seven, eight. Then the shoulders, keep them bouncy for now. Tense them up later, that's always important to add force, but right now we're just warming up the punch. Kick lightly too, she winced as she kicked out her right leg. Today we need to take it easy. Relax, have fun with it.

She knew she wouldn't. Thursday at five was many things to her, but a light, enjoyable workout was never one. Sure, she occasionally came into the class a bit fatigued after three hours of making lattes at the campus café and two and a half more crunching numbers for an upcoming statistics exam. But then the music started and the beat of the dance music pulsated through the walls, engulfing those trapped in the room. Just as it had that night. The underlying carnal boom-boom stirred deep in her, the angry thump of a bad dream vibrated across the floor and through her body. Jab cross. Kickboxing was never simple. And not fun.

"Give me a right hook!" Rachel called over the music. The front half of the class followed the demand but the back could not hear it above the volume of the speaker. Second time around they got it, and the group of 50 strong females moved in rhythm, in time. "Left elbow!" Punch. Elbow. Five, six, seven, eight. "Add a knee in there! Give it to him!" The class reached up to the ceiling, grabbed an imaginary perpetrator and pulled him to their uplifted knees. "Again!" Take that, Julie thought to herself, pulling down as hard as she could and throwing her knee into him with all her might.

"Now advance!" Together, they pushed up to the front of the room. Jab, jab, jab, cross. Then retreat, six, seven, eight. Jab, jab, jab, cross. Up and back, the flow of a united fight. Jab, jab, jab, cross. Step to the side, lean and kick out. Impact with the heel. Let him feel that, Julie whispered to herself, punching harder, kicking higher, seven, eight. Up. Together. Let them all feel that. Back. As one. Seven, eight.

Twenty-seven percent of women who are raped realize they are victims. The rest blame themselves.

And who speaks for them? She cursed silently as she punched again. What about those who don't know, don't understand, whose hearts sink down to the acidic base of their stomachs every time they remember what happened but still, still think it was their fault, that they got too carried away last Saturday night? I am the slut, they think. Still think. It's my fault. That's all I am good for.

Jab, jab, jab, cross. Some of the freshmen who were new to the class and university life seemed a bit unsure of themselves. They giggled at their own clumsiness when faced with the constant advancing, retreating, and the awkward high kicks. Several of them stumbled a bit as they found themselves being swept back and forth by the right-step-kicking, left-step-kicking around them. Others couldn't remember when exactly to start to pull back. But they watched closely, never taking their eyes from the calm coordination of the instructor, or the older girls in front of them. The juniors and seniors knew the moves, where to hit, how to hit, at what to aim. They punched at shadows and kicked at imaginary demons. Four, three, two, one. Julie's breath came quicker now, her moves more deliberate. Start over. Hook. Elbow. Again and again, the instinct imbedded with the throbbing music in their hearts.

Zero. How many times it is a woman's fault that she is raped.

At least, that was what the pamphlet said. She used to keep it in the back of her desk drawer, taking it out only late at night, locking her door so that none of her friends would wander in and see what her bedtime reading was. A woman was never to blame, the brochure read, never. It didn't matter if you shoved your tits up so high and close together that they looked like they would explode from your shirt at any minute, didn't matter if you literally strapped yourself to a catapult and flung yourself on a guy, and it didn't matter if you sneaked upstairs with him and didn't protest when he unhooked your bra.

"Four kicks forward! Five, six, seven, eight!" the instructor called. Julie kicked. Fifty women followed her. The beat pounded. The sweat poured. Their arms went back and forth. Side kick. Five, six, seven, eight. Now punch forward, kick back. Get the guy right there, in the stomach, or better yet a bit further down. Side again. Fight him off. Get rid of him. Get rid of it all. Make it go away. Forever.

Nine out of ten women don't report a rape.

And so what? What good would it do, anyway? Those pamphlets, those damn pamphlets tell you not to wash yourself (jab harder with that left, dammit!!), to stay away from the shower, to put all your clothes in a paper bag, not plastic (as if I was fucking coherent when it happened, hook and retreat!). That way, they can get the physical evidence. They can lay you out on a stretcher and expose you to the entire world and see if he left a hair behind.

Then they take you to a courtroom and before they let him off, have you listen in silence as he testifies, "She'd been asking for it the whole night." Elbow, six, seven, eight. You're all alone then, walking across the green lawns of campus and everyone looks at you disgustedly cause they think you're some dumb girl who laid the wrong guy and turned him in as a rapist. Knee! Or they try to give comfort when all they can offer you is their absolute horror of what has happened, and they can't even give you that because they can never ever understand. So they just talk to you for 20 minutes about how nice it is that it's been warmer than usual this spring and don't once look you in the eyes for the entire conversation. Yes. That was what I needed. Squat left!

At least report it anonymously, the pamphlet tells you, get the guy on record, get the incident down, do something. Squat right!

But they don't tell you about running across the black star-less night of a party-happy campus, up muddy fields and across littered sidewalks with your bra in your hands because you didn't want to take the time to put it on; you just wanted to get out of there and go anywhere else, anywhere else. They don't tell you about the way you lock your doors and close your windows and sit in the emptiness of your room thinking, "you slut, you slut, you slut." Don't wash! What about the hours you spend under the showerhead, the hours every day for weeks after, because all you want is to be clean and clean and you can't ever be clean again but all you know to do is keep using soap? Lunge right! And they don't tell you about the next day's jokes, the shit you take from your friends, the laughs about hooking up with so-and-so's cousin from Vermont the other night, and the winks and the giggles, and how you learn to shut off your eyes and laugh too, but you just want to die inside because the fact is that you are too numb and horrified to even admit to yourself what really happened, and it takes so long to find the courage to say just to yourself, "I was raped" that how can you ever begin to tell a sister or a best friend or a policeman and hand over your underwear in a lunch sack?

"Give me a no means no, ladies!"

Nine out of ten.

"NO MEANS NO!" The girls shouted at the memories that haunted the aerobics class. Step, swing that elbow around. Other side. Start again.

No means no! Julie wanted to scream, again and again, until her throat pulsed with pain and she lay out of breath on the polished wooden floor. It did mean no. It had fucking meant no. One no. That was all she should have needed. She'd done the math on that too many times before, she knew those numbers. And she knew she wasn't one of the other kinds of numbers, the made-up ones with soft, straight blond hair and perfect bodies who giggled "no" as they pulled him in and ended up as checkmarks on guys' to-screw lists. No. She was the faceless number left upstairs on the bed with si-lent unfalling tears. The one in four, the nine in ten, the en-lightened 27. The million.

"YAAHH!!" the entire class grunted collectively as they again shoved their knee into that imaginary perpetrator. Jab, jab, jab, cross. Five, six, seven, eight. "YAAHHH!" Take that, asshole. Step kick right, step kick left. And that! This is for you, Ryan. Take it and go.

84% of women know their assailants.

She knew only his eyes, those playful green globes that followed her around the party that night, urged her mischievously up the stairs, pulling her, teasing her along, and leading her to the room. The only light within came from a dying yellow streetlamp that shone through the window. The room smelled like athletic socks and heavy cologne, the bed was nothing more than a simple mattress on the floor with a sheet tossed carelessly across it.

She had stumbled in. The door locked behind her. Kick front.

Her heart beat faster as she turned, and saw him staring at her with a different expression in his eyes. Side kick. She drew in a quiet, shaky breath as the distance between her and him narrowed. Back. The light was still off.

She had to admit, she had still found him intriguing at this point, as he sat down with her on the mattress and traced his fingers up and down, and across her arm before finally coming to a rest on her hand and squeezing it reassuringly. Four jabs. The tips of his hair brushed against her forehead as he bent down to kiss her. Lightly, delicately, his lips seeking only acceptance. Four hooks and slide back.

How could she have refused that? So warm, so mysterious, so adventurous. She eagerly returned his embraces with her own, nipping her tongue around the caverns of his mouth, reveling in the twinge of danger. Uppercut. Deeper she delved into his mouth, craning further, reaching for more. Throw that elbow out there. Again. Seven, eight.

He felt her response, and continued further into the kiss, deeper, working in and down as if trying to surround her. A hand ran across the border between her tank-top and jeans, up to her breasts, back down to the hem of the shirt. Hand, cold hand stroked her stomach, her back, and slithered up as it felt for the special clasp hidden in back. Three knees, right.

And she played the game, yes she did, arching her body closer to his own, moaning gently as he explored her, running her fingers up, through his hair, across his back, and around to the side to stroke his neck. Three knees left. Then he shifted his weight forward, slowly, meticulously, and laid her out across the bed, feeling her jeans loosen around her waist as she stretched into that vulnerable position, and she still didn't stop him. Squat left, strike on the side.

Then he straddled her, took her slender hips between his two muscular legs, and she felt his full force pushed up against her, wanting too much. The shiver she felt before when he had shut the two of them off from the world returned, and warned her that she had gone too far. Squat, chop hard!

She tried to relax her lips, pull away, calm the energy pulsating from him. Cooler embraces, less touch, quench his thirst in a more chaste manner. He pressed down harder. Beneath his weight she struggled to draw her legs together. Lunge forward. "No!" the class shrieks. "No!"

She twisted and turned, but he is crouched between her legs. Bent over, face close to hers, he ripped her shirt over her head and threw it across the room, tears the bra away from her skin, breaking the clasps. Elbow, swing, elbow, swing. He dropped her down to the mattress. The sheet was cool against her back. She pulled her fingers from his hair and bent away, pushed against him, trying to get him to ease up, pull up, get up, stop, no means no. . . .

"Ryan, wait-" Grunting, he pulled her up again and wrapped one massive arm around her body, pinning her arms to her sides. The knotted sheet protruded into her back.

"Come on baby, don't you worry," he moaned in between hard kisses, leaning down farther, closer, the beer and the sweat and the heat overpowering her senses. Jump kick left. Jump kick right.

"No, look, I don't want—" One hand was sliding down the bed, winding around her waist, the button of her jeans, her zipper. "No, don't—" his cold hand wascaressing her down beneath her panties, pulling the cloth down to the base of her thighs.

"It's okay, it's okay," he sighed, his voice high, intent. A buckle falls against her abdomen, the cold metal a shock from the heat between them. Elbow, swing, again, out, away from it all, away. She inhaled sharply. "Sorry," he murmurs, tossing the belt to one side, reaching for the button of his own pants. Right elbow, left hook, knee. His eyes closed, his back arched, his face rising toward the ceiling. Around her, on top of her, rising up above like a diver ready to plummet into the water.

"No!" she whispered as he plunged in.

She did not move, could not move, her legs trapped by her jeans now sweaty and sticking to her skin, her arms imprisoned on either side of her body, the weight of his desire forcing her down, beating, tearing, pulsing with "huh-huh-huh" breaths. She lay there, lay there, frozen in the heat of his in-out-in-out while his eyes glowed overhead. The music pounded. She closed her eyes.

"Are you ready for one more?" Rachel's voice called. It was 5:57 already, but Julie's 88th class still left one last opportunity to fight back. If I only had one more, she thought ruefully, but I guess I will just have to take my revenge with this. She smiled grimly in the mirror. That's what I want, that's all I want. But for now, here's to you, Ryan, she thought as she pulled herself back into the ready position.

"Go get him, girls! Give it all you got!" The beat started. The women began.

All we got. All I got. Right hook. Left elbow. This is for that so-called harmless flirting all night. Reach up, pull down, knee to chest. Take that! For the way you left me curled up on the mattress when you went back down to the party! Advance, jab, jab, jab, cross. That and that and that and that! Retreat. Right step, kick. For making me lie awake at night, too ashamed to cry. Left step, kick. The ashtrays full of hopeless cigarettes! The stink of empty whisky glasses I didn't even bother rinsing out any more. Front kick, kick, kick, kick. I can never, never, never, never forgive this! Kick right, left, right, left.

Back, six, seven, eight. Never, never, never, never get over this! Jab forward, two, three, four. Hook back, six, seven, eight. And never, ever, leave it behind! Uppercut, uppercut, elbow, elbow. And I wish you could feel that. Jump kick right! Jump kick left! Cause I still feel you. When I walk across campus I feel you. When I turn away from another pleasant conversation with a guy, I feel you. When I look in the mirror, I see you there, forever. Reach up, pull you down on my knee. I want you to cry. I want you to suffer. I want you to agonize over me every waking hour of the day. Just as I do you. Squat left, side chop. "No!" Squat right, side chop. "No!" Lunge front, punch. "No!" Again. "No!"

And step, elbow, step, elbow, swing out and around and all at you, again and again and again in repetition, endless infinite repetition, Ryan, and endless perpetual hate from me and infinite pain and everlasting hell to you because no means no means no means no means no . . .

She stood outside the gym, away from the movement, the sweat, the throbbing dance beats. She leaned against the brick wall, massaging her sore right leg, watching the swarms of girls leave the studio, head off to meals, to parties, to boyfriends and lives after kickboxing. Fourteen, she counted. Final figure.

Turning, she trudged off into the gray twilight. The cold breeze whipped her hair behind her and nipped around her bare legs, numbing her in the late November evening. Alone again, alone and nothing to do but make her way across the frozen, muddy lawns to her solitary room. One in four, she thought as she plodded up the hill. Nine in ten. One more week till one more fight. Again.

The last brown leaves rustled in the distance, the smiling faces were far away in brightly lit buildings. She paused, watching the sickly yellow streetlights flicker on, the black trees stretch out to the sky, and the darkness enveloping them all. "No," she whispered one last time. It was stolen away from her on the wind.

ABOUT THE AUTHORS

Jennifer Lawler

Jennifer, a second-degree black belt in Tae Kwon Do, teaches personal safety and martial arts workshops throughout the country. She has written more than 25 published books, including the *Dojo Wisdom* series (Penguin Compass), *Martial Arts for Dummies* (Wiley), *Tae Kwon Do for Women*, *Kickboxing for Women* (with Debz Buller; both from Wish Publishing) and *The Self Defense Deck* (Chronicle Books).

She has written on the relationship between martial arts and personal growth for magazines as diverse as *Family Circle, Cooking Light, Black Belt, Martial Arts, Weight Watchers, Women's Circle,* and *American Fitness* and has written for online sites such as eHow about martial arts and self-defense. She is frequently interviewed in print and on the radio as a martial arts expert. She is the editor of the quarterly martial arts magazine of the American Taekwondo Association, *ATA World.*

A former college English teacher, she earned her doctorate in English from the University of Kansas.

She lives in the Midwest with her adorable daughter Jessica and a mutt of indeterminate origin and lazy disposition.

For more information about Jennifer and her books, visit www.jenniferlawler.com

Laura Kamienski

Laura holds the rank of third dan in the Korean martial art of Tae Kwon Do. Along with being named International Tae Kwon Do Union Instructor of the Year, Woman of the Year and being recognized for her outstanding contribution to martial arts, her awards include three exemplary achievement medallions, which she earned for forms presentation and sparring.

Laura is the founder and head instructor of Kicks Martial Arts for Women in Lewisburg, Pennsylvania. She is the Pennsylvania State Director of the International Tae Kwon Do Union and a certified self-defense instructor with the National Women's Martial Arts Federation. Ms. Kamienski is the creator of Empower! Self-Defense for Women, a multistrategy feminist self-defense course focusing on the specific needs and concerns of women and girls.

She has been a group fitness and aerobics instructor for over a decade and is the creator of CardioKicks!, a fitness kickboxing program that combines practical martial arts techniques and empowering elements of women's self-defense with the excitement and fun of traditional aerobic classes.

Her articles have appeared in such publications as *ATA World*, *Women in the Martial Arts*, and Feminista.com. She is currently pursuing a graduate degree in philosophy.

For more information about Laura Kamienski or Kicks Martial Arts for Women, please visit *www.Kicks4Women.com*.